TRE

Counterfeit Christs

Finding the Real Jesus Among the Impostors

Catholic Answers Press

Published by Catholic Answers, Inc.
2020 Gillespie Way
El Cajon, California 92020
1-888-291-8000 orders
619-387-0042 fax
catholic.com

Printed in the United States of America

Cover and interior design by Russell Graphic Design

978-1-68357-116-2
978-1-68357-117-9 Kindle
978-1-68357-118-6 ePub

Jesus, I Trust in You

CONTENTS

Counterfeits from Ideologues

Counterfeits from Protestants

INTRODUCTION

It was a crisp morning at the University of New Mexico, where I was engaging in pro-life evangelism. At the time, the campus medical school was teaching students how to perform abortions, so the images of aborted children we displayed garnered a fairly hostile response from the campus population. One student's response still sticks out in my mind.

After angrily arguing with us in the morning, he returned in the afternoon wearing a tunic and fake beard. He then shouted as loud as he could, "Don't do this in my name! Don't do this in my name!"

"And who are you supposed to be?" I asked.

"You know me. I am your master and I demand you stop imposing your values on other people. It offends me!"

"Oh!" I said with enthusiasm. "You must be Jesus. I'm a huge fan but I have a question. You love everyone, right?"

"You shall love your neighbor as yourself!" he shouted back as loud as he could.

"Right, so are babies in the womb my neighbor? If I'm supposed to love unborn children, shouldn't I try to get people to stop killing them?"

He looked at me for a second, turned around, and walked away shouting over and over again, "Not in my name! Not in my name!"

It's funny that this man didn't condemn Jesus along with Christians who stand up for the unborn. Instead, he believed that if Jesus were really present he would have agreed with him that *we* were the problem, not abortionists.

It seems like everyone wants to have Jesus on "their side." Sometimes, people are willing even to ignore or re-write history in order to make that happen.

For example, in 1813 Thomas Jefferson composed *The Life and Morals of Jesus of Nazareth* (later known as the Jefferson Bible) by using a razor to cut out sections of the New Testament that, in his view, described the *real* Jesus. Jefferson was a deist who rejected the idea of God intervening in the world, so the miraculous parts of the New Testament ended up on a literal cutting-room floor. What remained was the story of a wise moral teacher who was tragically killed and then buried in a tomb.

Jefferson would not be the only explorer in what would later be called "the quest for the historical Jesus." These "questers" came to include both scholars and popular sensationalists claiming to have discovered the identity of the "historical Jesus" who became obscured by the traditional "Christ of faith" worshipped by Christians. But *is* the Christ of faith a mere fantasy that must yield to what historical research says about Jesus? Or is the Jesus whom Christians worship the same person as the Jewish carpenter who lived in Palestine 2,000 years ago?

This is an essential question, because the foundation of our eternal salvation is rooted in events related to the birth, life, death, and resurrection of Jesus of Nazareth. As Pope Benedict XVI wrote, "For biblical faith the historicity—and thus the 'facticity'—of the Incarnation is indispensable. Faith demands that we consider Jesus as approachable by historical research."[1]

St. Paul agreed that our faith must be rooted in fact. As he declared to the Christians in Corinth: "If Christ has not been raised, your faith is futile and you are still in your sins" (1 Cor. 15:17).

In this book I have set out to show how historical research and sound biblical exegesis refute the many incorrect views people have about Jesus Christ—the phony, fictional, *counterfeit* versions of Jesus that they have devised for their own ends. Entire books have been written on some of these counterfeits, but my goal is to identify and expose these impostors in a brief and straightforward way that everyone can understand.

We'll organize these different views of Jesus according to groups of people who share similar beliefs.

First, there are the *non-religious,* who believe Jesus was just a non-judgmental teacher whose real life story was replaced with later legends. Among these people are committed atheists, some of whom take pride in trying to show Jesus never even existed at all.

But even among *religious people* you can find plenty of counterfeit Christs. These include the Jesus of non-Christians religions like Islam, Buddhism, and Hinduism—a Jesus who may be a wise teacher, even a prophet sent by God, but is himself not God incarnate. This group also includes members of "quasi-Christian" religions, like Jehovah's Witnesses, Mormons, and Oneness Pentecostals, who deny essential elements of the traditional Christian faith.

Some people object to the idea that one group of Christians can define who is and who is not a Christian, but even atheists like the late Christopher Hitchens agreed that in order for the word *Christian* to be meaningful it must relate to specific supernatural claims regarding Jesus Christ.

For example, in 2012 Unitarian Universalist Marilyn Sewell interviewed Hitchens and chided him for not engaging more "liberal Christianity." Sewell considers herself a Christian and believes that Jesus was merely a model of social justice and that salvation is a metaphor for how one can go from "being dead to the world and dead to other people, and can be resurrected to new life." In response, Hitchens bluntly said, "If you don't believe that Jesus of Nazareth was the Christ and Messiah, and that he rose again from the dead and by his sacrifice our sins are forgiven, you're really not in any meaningful sense a Christian."[2]

I would add that belief in the atonement and in Jesus' resurrection are certainly necessary conditions for being Christian, but they aren't sufficient. At a bare minimum, a Christian is someone who has received a valid baptism and believes in the Trinity. When it comes to Jesus, this means believing that he is one divine person who fully possesses two natures: one human and the other divine. According to the *Catechism of the Catholic Church* (CCC):

> Christ's human nature belongs, as his own, to the divine person of the Son of God, who assumed it. Everything that Christ is and does in this nature derives from "one of the Trinity." The Son of God therefore communicates to his humanity his own personal mode of existence in the Trinity. In his soul as in his body, Christ thus expresses humanly the divine ways of the Trinity (470).

Nearly all of the counterfeit Christs we examine in this book have their origin in a denial of Jesus' identity as an eternal, divine person with a fully divine nature who became man by assuming a fully human nature through the Incarnation. But some of these counterfeits err, not in their Christology, but in their decision to hitch the real Jesus to a moral or theological error or ideology. These include moral errors like the affirmation of homosexual behavior and communism as well as theological errors like prosperity theology, Calvinistic determinism, and the denial of Christ's presence in the Eucharist.

To put it plainly, if you get Jesus wrong, there's nothing of equal importance to "get right" that can make up for such an error. That's why I pray the Holy Spirit will use the evidence in this book to both prevent people from abandoning our Lord and also break the hold any of these counterfeit Christs may have over souls that need to know our true God and Savior, Jesus Christ (Titus 2:13).

COUNTERFEITS
from the Non-Religious

1

Non-Judgmental Buddy

I had just finished giving a talk to a group of Catholic schoolteachers and I could tell it wasn't well received. Many of them folded their arms, looked down at their phones, or just scowled at me.

What had I done to earn this response?

When one of the attendees asked me about how to teach the concept of mortal sin to high school students, I said: "First, mortal sin involves grave matter. This includes actions like murder, rape, adultery . . ." So far everyone was in agreement, but then I added, "as well as abortion, contraception, and sexual activity in an invalid marriage."

At that, more than half the teachers rolled their eyes, scoffed, or made some gesture to let me know they thought I was out of line (once again, this was a Catholic high school!). Afterward, I asked one of teachers, "What did you think of my presentation?"

"No offense," she said, "but people like you get worked up about minor things like who can and can't receive

Communion, whereas I think we should just focus on being people of faith."

"Well," I replied, "the Church does teach that you shouldn't receive the Eucharist if you are in a state of mortal sin. It's a serious matter," I replied.

"I just don't think *Jesus* would say that," she continued. "He wouldn't say, 'No, you can't have this because of somebody's rules.' Jesus would be compassionate, not judgmental."

I noticed on her nametag that she taught *theology*, but I wasn't surprised. Most people, including many Catholics, think of Jesus as being merely a friend or a "buddy." Even if Jesus is "God" or the "Son of God," he's not a demanding deity who would call us a bunch of "sinners."

The real sin, according to these people, is calling someone else a sinner or being "judgmental." After all, if Jesus said, "Judge not" (Matt. 7:1) then shouldn't Christians stop pointing out other people's sins?

But how can that be true if . . .

. . . Jesus Never Completely Forbade Judgment

People who say, "Jesus would never judge anyone" or "Jesus wouldn't say something harsh like that" have never carefully read the Bible. Jesus condemned hypocritical and inaccurate judgments, but we know he could not have condemned *judgment itself* because he taught the crowds the *right way* to judge! "Do not judge by appearances, but judge with right judgment" (John 7:24).

We don't know the invisible content of someone's soul, so we can't ever say with certainty if he is in a state of grace or not. That's why St. Paul tells us not to "pronounce judgment before the time, before the Lord comes, who will bring to light the things now hidden in darkness and will disclose the purposes of the heart" (1 Cor. 4:5). We can, however, judge the visible content of human actions and determine if they are good or evil.

If we couldn't do that, then we could never say *any* act is wrong—including the act of judging other people's actions! So we should judge whether people's actions are right or wrong, but not in order to make ourselves feel morally superior to them. *That* is the attitude Jesus condemned when he said, "Judge not, that you be not judged." If we judge other people's sins, then we must take care because that same judgment will come upon us (and possibly in a harsher way) if we commit those same sins (Matt. 7:2).

Instead, we should judge people's actions out of love and concern for those who sin and lead others into sin. It is only through correct judgment that we can identify which actions might keep that person (and ourselves) from spending eternity with God and then urge the person to repent and change his life.

Jesus began his ministry by proclaiming, "The kingdom of God is at hand; repent, and believe in the gospel" (Mark 1:15) and he didn't sugarcoat his message about the sins from which people needed to repent. For example, he publicly called the religious leaders of his day "fools," "blind guides," and "hypocrites" who are like "whitewashed tombs, which outwardly appear beautiful, but within they are full of dead men's bones and all uncleanness" (Matt. 23:27).

Jesus' harsh words to the Pharisees and even his own disciples (like when he called Peter "Satan" in Matthew 16:23) were not petty insults but serious wake-up calls. His judgment of sin is more like the diagnosis of a doctor who wants to give the patient a cure than the sentence of a judge who only wants to enforce the law. That's why Jesus said, "I did not come to judge the world but to save the world" (John 12:47) and, "For judgment I came into this world, that those who do not see may see, and that those who see may become blind" (John 7:24).

When the Pharisees criticized Jesus' decision to dine with notorious sinners like prostitutes, Jesus did not chastise them for being "judgmental." Their error was not in caring too much about sin but in not caring enough about *sinners*. Jesus reminded them, "Those who are well have no need of a physician, but those who are sick; I came not to call the righteous, but sinners" (Mark 2:17). According to New Testament professor Robert Gagnon:

> What was distinctive about Jesus' ministry was not that he refused to make judgments about the conduct of others, or even that he lowered his moral standards. On the contrary, in many areas he elevated those standards. What was distinctive was his incredibly generous spirit even toward those who had lived in gross disobedience to God for years. He expended enormous effort and exhibited great compassion in the search for the lost. Jesus did not wait for the lost to come to him. He went looking for them.[3]

. . . Jesus Is Our Judge

In response to the theology teacher who claimed Jesus wouldn't say of the Eucharist, "No, you can't have this because of somebody's rules," I gently pointed out what Jesus said in Matthew 7:6: "Do not give dogs what is holy; and do not throw your pearls before swine, lest they trample them under foot and turn to attack you." In this case, Jesus was talking precisely about *not* giving precious, holy things to people who have no intention of recognizing their value.

In fact, a first-century catechism called the *Didache* instructs Christians to remember, "Let no one eat or drink of your Thanksgiving (Eucharist), but they who have been baptized into the name of the Lord; for concerning this also the Lord has said, give not that which is holy to the dogs" (9).

This is not done out of selfish pride but selfless concern for people who might abuse that which is holy and further alienate himself from God. St. Paul warned that whoever "eats the bread or drinks the cup of the Lord in an unworthy manner will be guilty of profaning the body and blood of the Lord" (1 Cor. 11:27). To avoid this, he advises Christians to discern and judge themselves, noting that "if we judged ourselves truly, we should not be judged. But when we are judged by the Lord, we are chastened so that we may not be condemned along with the world" (1 Cor. 11:31–32).

The ultimate refutation of the non-judgmental counterfeit Christ is Jesus' own promise that he would judge the entire world.

Jesus said that at the end of time, "When the Son of Man comes in his glory, and all the angels with him, then he will sit on his glorious throne. Before him will be gathered all the nations, and he will separate them one from another as a shepherd separates the sheep from the goats" (Matt. 25:31–32). This separation involves judging people to see if they were among the sheep who followed God's will or if they were among the goats who rejected it. Jesus says the latter will "go away into eternal punishment, but the righteous into eternal life" (Matt. 25:46).

In another instance, Jesus made it abundantly clear what the fate of the damned would be like:

Just as the weeds are gathered and burned with fire, so will it be at the close of the age. The Son of Man will send his angels, and they will gather out of his kingdom all causes of sin and all evildoers, and throw them into the furnace of fire; there men will weep and gnash their teeth (Matt. 13:40–42).

I'm always amused when non-religious people condemn the "wrathful" God of the Old Testament and say they prefer "meek and mild" Jesus. Whereas everlasting damnation is only hinted at in the Old Testament, it is explicitly taught in the New. Jesus even said the punishment that awaited the unrepentant inhabitants of Capernaum would be worse than the fiery destruction God rained down upon the sinful cities of Sodom and Gomorrah in the book of Genesis (Matt. 11:23).

That's why I appreciate outspoken atheists like Dan Barker who call Jesus a "tyrant" and "lunatic."[4] Jesus would indeed be a megalomaniacal basket case if he thought he could "play God" and judge the entire world—unless Jesus really was God. This is why C.S. Lewis thought Jesus might have been "lunatic" but that he couldn't possibly have been just a wise, merely human teacher:

> A man who was merely a man and said the sort of things Jesus said would not be a great moral teacher. He would either be a lunatic—on the level with the man who says he is a poached egg—or else he would be the Devil of Hell . . . You can shut him up for a fool, you can spit at him and kill him as a demon or you can fall at his feet and call him Lord and God, but let us not come with any patronizing nonsense about his being a great human teacher. He has not left that open to us. He did not intend to.[5]

. . . Jesus Is Our Lord

Some people object to the idea that Jesus claimed to be God because Jesus never simply declared, "I am God, worship me!" But Jesus *did* allow people to worship him and call him God (John 20:28) and the Jewish people wanted to execute him for making himself equal with God (John 5:18). Indeed, if Jesus were just a charismatic rabbi who preached love, mercy, and forgiveness, then why would anyone want to crucify him?

In John 8:56, Jesus told the Jewish leaders, "Your father Abraham rejoiced that he was to see my day; he saw it and was glad." This understandably puzzled them because Abraham had died more than a thousand years earlier. "You are not yet fifty years old, and have you seen Abraham?" they said. To which Jesus responded, "Before Abraham was, I AM."[6]

The next verse says the people "took up stones to throw at [Jesus]" so he wasn't just making an eccentric statement about being really old. Rather, he was taking God's sacred name, which was first revealed to Moses (I AM WHO I AM), and applying it to himself. This name was so sacred it couldn't even be written down, and it was later replaced in writing with the Hebrew word for "Lord."

In this one declaration, Jesus affirmed that he existed *eternally* before Abraham, which sent the high priests into a frenzy and motivated them to kill Jesus for blasphemy (John 8:59). Biblical scholars Robert Bowman and J. Ed Komosewski say this reaction from Jesus' audience "confirms that they thought he was making a divine claim."[7]

Some critics respond that these kinds of claims are only found in John's Gospel, which was the last to be written. According to them, Jesus' divinity was a later legend that supplanted stories about a merely human Jesus (a hypothesis we will further debunk in the next few chapters).[8]

It is true the earlier Gospels emphasize Jesus' humanity more than John's Gospel, but that doesn't mean they denied Jesus' divine nature.

For example, in those Gospels Jesus implicitly affirmed his divine identity by gathering twelve disciples, who symbolized the twelve tribes of Israel. Rather than representing one of the tribes himself, such as the tribe of Levi (which had a claim to the priesthood), Jesus stood apart from the twelve disciples, and gathered them together in the same way that God called the twelve tribes of Israel.

In Mark 12, Jesus shared a parable about a vineyard whose wicked tenants kill the servants the owner has sent. The parable is similar to other illustrations from the prophets, who identified the vineyard with Israel and the servants with the prophets Israel previously rejected (Isa. 5). But in Jesus' parable, the owner's last action is to send his *son*, whom the wicked tenants also kill. Notice how Jesus identifies himself not with a *servant* of the vineyard owner (that is, one of the human prophets), but with the owner's *son*.[9] Just as the son of the vineyard owner was killed because of his relationship to the father, so too would Jesus be killed because of his claim to having a special and unique relationship with the heavenly Father.

Jesus also spoke of a relationship with God that was unlike what any human being shared with the divine when he said, "All things have been delivered to me by my Father; and no one knows the Son except the Father, and no one knows the Father except the Son and any one to whom the Son chooses to reveal him" (Matt. 11:27).

Finally, when Jesus refers to himself as the "Son of Man" he is not denying his divine sonship but applying a messianic title from the book of Daniel that would not be appropriate for a mere human being. Daniel has a vision of heaven and says:

I saw in the night visions, and behold, with the clouds of heaven there came one like a Son of Man, and he came to the Ancient of Days and was presented before him. And to him was given dominion and glory and kingdom, that all peoples, nations, and languages should serve him; his dominion is an everlasting dominion, which shall not pass away, and his kingdom one that shall not be destroyed (7:13–14).

So, if Jesus was too moral to be a liar and too sane to be a lunatic, then he must have been the Lord.[10] Right?

Not so fast. The agnostic New Testament scholar Bart Ehrman says that "there could be a fourth option—legend."[11] Perhaps later generations of Christians, or even the ruling secular powers, manufactured stories about Jesus claiming to be divine and performing miracles. This theory forms the basis for our next counterfeit.

Victim of Conspiracies

During a prayer meeting I led for our local youth group a girl came up to me with a copy of *The Da Vinci Code* (DVC). She asked, "Have you read this? It has really shaken my faith!"

I glanced it over and said, "It's just a novel, right? Why does it bother you?"

"Because the author says that his story is based on real facts about the Catholic Church. Like how the Church hid the Gospels that told the real story about Jesus."

I'd heard these kinds of claims before, so I promised her that by our next meeting I'd get her "the rest of the story." I read the DVC over the following weekend and what stuck out to me most was not the book's formulaic plot or lackluster characters. It was instead the sheer number of brazen falsehoods in a book that begins with this preface: "FACT: All descriptions of artwork, architecture, documents, and secret rituals in this novel are accurate."

At our next meeting, instead of debunking every single inaccuracy I just focused on the most important and inaccurate claim made by the novel's historian character Sir Leigh Teabing: Jesus was just a wise teacher, and belief in his divinity did not occur to anyone until the Roman emperor

Constantine mandated it at the Council of Nicaea in A.D. 325. He also claims there were other Gospels that were "outlawed, gathered up, and burned" because they told this "real story" about Jesus.[12]

This means all we have been left with today is a story about a Jesus who claimed to be divine and rose from the dead that was made up to replace the real story of a merely human teacher.

But how can that be true if . . .

. . . The Conspiracy Is Impossible

Teabing makes it sound like Emperor Constantine just walked into a few churches, gathered up all the documents that would foil his plans, and then quietly destroyed them without anyone noticing. But the number of ancient manuscripts and the size of the ancient Church would make such a feat impossible.

Even if all the Gospels were gathered up and destroyed, that wouldn't remove them from the memory of the Christians who had heard them and cared about them passionately. St. Augustine once told St. Jerome that the people of Tripoli rioted in the streets because Jerome's new translation of the book of Jonah was so unfamiliar to them.[13] Now, consider that Christians comprised between seven and ten percent of the Roman Empire in the year 300, some three to four million people.[14] Imagine what these millions of people would have done if Constantine presented a completely new story about Christ to them! It's inconceivable that they would all abandon their faith in the "mortal Jesus" in favor of this new Imperial belief system without leaving a trace.

Destroying the Gospels also wouldn't erase their existence from the voluminous writings of the Church Fathers—the

Christian writers and leaders of the first few centuries. The critical author Bart Ehrman admits that, when it comes to the Church Father's quotations of the New Testament, "so extensive are these citations that if all other sources for our knowledge of the text of the New Testament were destroyed, they would be sufficient alone for the reconstruction of practically the entire New Testament."[15]

But the reality is that the fourth-century Church could never have destroyed all the Gospels that were in circulation at that time.

There currently exist over 5,000 copies of New Testament manuscripts written in Greek, and over 9,000 manuscripts written in other languages like Latin, Coptic, and Syriac.[16] Sixty-nine of the Greek manuscripts can be dated to within 250 years of the original copies,[17] suggesting that there were hundreds or even thousands more in circulation at the time that, like ninety-nine percent of all ancient manuscripts, were later lost.[18]

Furthermore, no one was ever in a position to gather up all the New Testament manuscripts and replace or destroy them. If it took the United States government ten years and extensive satellite surveillance to find Osama Bin Laden hiding in a cave in Afghanistan, how much better could Constantine's minions do in trying to find hundreds of manuscripts hidden in similar caves in the ancient world?

Finally, we should note that the first complete copy of the New Testament, called the *Codex Sinaiticus* (because it was discovered in a monastery at the foot of Mount Sinai), can be dated to within 300 years of the original documents. Compare this to Homer's *Iliad*, which was written in the eighth century B.C. Although a few fragments of the *Iliad* can be dated to within 500 years of Homer, the oldest

complete copy of the *Iliad* was written in the tenth century
A.D., or 1,800 years later!

Biblical scholar F. F. Bruce puts it bluntly: "There is no
body of ancient literature in the world which enjoys such a
wealth of good textual attestation as the New Testament."[19]

. . . The Apocryphal Gospels Are Not Reliable

Many people think there are only four Gospels: Matthew,
Mark, Luke, and John. It's true that there are only four *canonical* Gospels—accounts of Christ's life that the Church
recognizes to be the inspired word of God. But in the decades and centuries that followed these accounts, other Gospels appeared that claimed to record the life of Christ. These
apocryphal texts include the Gospel of Peter, the Gospel of
Philip, and the Gospel of Mary Magdalene, among many
others.

According to the DVC, "Constantine commissioned and
financed a new Bible, which omitted those [apocryphal]
Gospels that spoke of Christ's *human* traits and embellished
those Gospels that made him godlike."[20]

Actually, the reverse is true.

The first-century canonical Gospels, like Matthew and
John, emphasize that Jesus was fully *man*: he experienced
hunger (Mark 11:12), ate food (Luke 24:43), shed tears (John
11:35), suffered to the point of sweating blood (Luke 22:44),
and died on a cross (John 19:30). It was a later heresy called
Docetism that claimed Jesus only *looked* human. According
to the Docetists, Christ's humanity was like a costume that
he, as God the Son, put on for our sake after he came down
to earth.

In his letter to the Smyrneans, St. Ignatius of Antioch
curtly rebuffed the Docetists by saying of Jesus, "He suffered

truly, even as also he truly raised up himself, not, as certain unbelievers maintain, that he only seemed to suffer, as they themselves only seem to be [Christians]."[21]

Even though the apocryphal Gospels vary considerably from the canonical Gospels in their description of Christ's earthly ministry, none of them actually support the DVC's conspiracy theory that Jesus was married to Mary Magdalene and that his descendants went on to form a powerful dynasty. The closest they come to saying this is in a difficult-to-decipher passage in the Gospel of Philip, which says of Mary Magdalene that Jesus "loved her more than all the disciples, and used to kiss her often on her mouth."

Even if the Gospel of Philip *did* say that Jesus was married to Mary Magdalene, it was written 200 years after the apostle Philip died, so it's not a reliable record of Christ's life.[22] Harvard professor Karen King notably did not appeal to this text in making her arguments that Jesus was married (she says it was probably a kiss of fellowship and not a romantic kiss). Instead, she presented to scholars what seemed to be an ancient Egyptian manuscript that contained the phrase, "Jesus said to them, 'my wife . . . " But that document turned out to be a medieval forgery.[23]

The apocryphal Gospels contain scenes that certainly make for entertaining reading. One example is the Gospel of Thomas's description of how a five-year-old Jesus made clay doves come to life, killed a child who was mean to him and then (thankfully) brought the child back from the dead. But when it comes to historical reliability they are, in the words of New Testament scholar Craig Blomberg, "little more than an artificial framework for imparting Gnostic doctrine."[24]

Gnosticism, which comes from the Greek word for knowledge (*gnosis*), claimed that an inferior deity created the evil material world. Humanity's salvation, therefore, comes not from the death and resurrection of God-made-man but from obtaining *secret knowledge* about how to unite with the superior deity that created the good spiritual world. This is evident in the opening lines of the Gospel of Thomas: "Whoever discovers the interpretation of these sayings will not taste death," in contrast with the real Jesus, who said in John 8:51, "If anyone keeps my word, he will never see death."

The first Christians rejected these Gnostic heresies and affirmed that Jesus Christ was fully God and fully man. In A.D. 110, Ignatius of Antioch wrote, "For our God, Jesus Christ, was, according to the appointment of God, conceived in the womb by Mary, of the seed of David, but by the Holy Ghost."[25] Thirty years later, the Christian writer Aristedes wrote, "God came down from heaven, and from a Hebrew virgin assumed and clothed himself with flesh."[26]

These Church Fathers, along with the other early witnesses of the Christian faith, taught the full humanity and divinity of Christ centuries before Emperor Theodosius declared Christianity the official religion of the Roman Empire in A.D. 381.

This brings us to the last piece of evidence that debunks conspiracies like those found in *The Da Vinci Code*.

. . . Belief in Jesus' Divinity Existed for Centuries Before Constantine

One of the earliest evidences for Christian belief in the divinity of Christ comes from the letters of the New Testament. Paul says that Jesus Christ is the "image of the invisible God" (Col. 1:15), in whom "the whole fullness of deity dwells bodily" (2:8–9). But some people who deny Christ's divinity translate Colossians 2:9, "For in him the fullness of *the divine quality* dwells bodily [emphasis added]."

To say Jesus has the fullness of *divine quality* instead of *divinity* could mean that Jesus is *like* God but not fully God. But Paul doesn't use the Greek word that means "divine quality" (*theiotes*) in this passage. He instead uses the Greek word *theotes,* which means that the very essence of the thing in question is God.[27] Paul also says in Titus 2:13 that we are "awaiting our blessed hope, the appearing of the glory of our great God and Savior Jesus Christ" (Titus 2:13).

In response, some critics claim that Titus 2:13 should be translated "wait for the happy hope and glorious manifestation of the great God and of our Savior, Jesus Christ," which implies that only the title *Savior* belongs to Jesus and not *great God.* But although it is true that humans can be saviors in a limited sense, only God can save humanity from sin, which is the salvation being talked about in this verse (see v.11). Furthermore, both *God* and *Savior* apply to Jesus in Titus 2:13 because of a rule in Greek grammar called Granville Sharp's Rule.[28] Basically, this rule applies in the following circumstances:

1. You have two nouns that are not proper names.
2. The first noun has an article in front of it but the second does not.
3. Both nouns are connected by the word *and* (in Greek, *kai*).

In 2 Peter 1:11 we see the rule applied in the following passage: "So there will be richly provided for you an entrance into the eternal kingdom of our Lord and Savior Jesus Christ." In this case, *Lord* and *Savior* are not proper names; the Greek word translated as *Lord* has an article but the Greek word translated as *Savior* does not; and both words are connected by the word *and.* We can conclude from Sharp's

Rule that both *Lord* and *Savior* refer to the same person: Jesus Christ. Since Titus 2:13 has an almost identical sentence structure to 2 Peter 1:11, why not translate it the same way and say that Jesus is both our Savior and our "great God?"

At this point some people might ask, "How do you know these references weren't just added to the New Testament centuries later?" Well, aside from the ancient biblical manuscript evidence, we have citations from *enemies* of the Church that corroborate Christian worship of Jesus.

Pliny the Younger, the second-century governor of the Roman province of Bythinia, interrogated Christians who refused to sacrifice to the gods. In a letter to Emperor Trajan he observed that Christians "were in the habit of meeting on a certain fixed day before it was light, when they sang in alternate verse a hymn to Christ as to a god, and bound themselves to a solemn oath."

Lucian of Samosata was a second-century playwright who thought Christians were gullible and ignorant fools. In his work *The Passing of Peregrinnus* he says that Christians "have sinned by denying the Greek gods, and by worshipping that crucified sophist himself and living according to his laws." A third-century drawing called the "Alexamanos graffito" even shows a Roman soldier worshipping a man with a donkey head being crucified. The drawing's caption reads, "Alexamanos worships [his] God."

Finally, one of my favorite whoppers in the DVC occurs when Teabing claims, "Jesus' establishment as 'the Son of God' was officially proposed and voted on by the Council of Nicaea." Another character responds, "Hold on. You're saying that Jesus' divinity was the result of a vote?"

"A relatively close one at that," Teabing replies.[29] But according to Bible critic Bart Ehrman, "There certainly was no vote to determine Jesus' divinity: this was already a matter of common knowledge among Christians, and had been from the early years of the religion."[30]

At Nicaea, the bishops were voting on how Jesus' divinity should be understood and expressed, not on whether he was divine at all. They asked, "Was Jesus *equal* in divinity with the Father or just *similar* in divinity to the Father?" The result of the final vote yielded 316 bishops in favor of the view that Jesus is equal in divinity with the Father and none in favor with the view that he is similar, while two abstained from voting.[31]

So the vote at Nicaea was indeed "relatively close"—to being a unanimous affirmation of the orthodox Catholic faith.

But how do we know that the Gospel accounts that informed the bishops' decisions were accurate in the first place? Let's now examine the claim that, even if "the real Jesus" wasn't purposefully hidden from us by an ancient conspiracy, perhaps he was simply lost to "the sands of time instead."

3

Man of Mystery

C.S. Lewis once said that one of the greatest obstacles to Christianity is not that the Bible contains miraculous accounts, but that it contains *ancient* ones. He writes of modern man:

> In his mind the present occupies almost the whole field of vision. Beyond it, isolated from it, and quite unimportant, is something called "The Old Days"—a small, comic jungle in which highwaymen, Queen Elizabeth, knights-in-armor, etc., wander about . . . [modern man] is "science," not "history," [which] is therefore felt to be much more real than The Old Days.[32]

If you've ever played the children's game of Telephone, you know how quickly a message can become distorted after it gets relayed through many people. Perhaps the same thing happened to the story of Jesus as the Bible was copied over and over again throughout the centuries.

The skeptic D.M. Murdock insists that the first retellings of the Gospel stories could not have been accurate because the Gospels themselves are unreliable. She writes, "Not only are the Gospels anonymous but also the dates at which they unmistakably emerge in the historical record are far too late for them to serve as the writings of 'eyewitnesses' or even companions to eyewitnesses."[33]

Given these circumstances, there's allegedly no way for us to separate historical facts about Jesus from later pious fictions designed to instill faith in Christ. This counterfeit Christ embodies modern skepticism that claims the real Jesus is buried under pious fictions that can never be separated from historical facts.

But how can that be true if...
. . . The Gospels Have Known Authors

A layperson might be puzzled at the idea that the Gospels are anonymous. After all, doesn't it say right at the top of each one, "The Gospel according to Matthew"—or Mark, or Luke, or John?

But skeptics claim that these titles were added later to the Gospel manuscripts and that the Gospels themselves do not identify who wrote them. For example, the *Cambridge Companion to the Gospels* says of Mark's Gospel, "Like the other New Testament Gospels, this one is anonymous. The author makes no self-reference within the narrative by which we might identify him, nor has he 'signed' his account. The title "The Gospel according to Mark" was added subsequent to the Gospel's completion."[34]

It's true that the Gospel texts didn't originally come with bylines. But many documents in the ancient world, including ones modern critics consider to be trustworthy, are also technically anonymous. The works of ancient Roman historian Tacitus do not bear his name, but very few historians have ever questioned that Tacitus wrote the *Annals*.[35] We know

Tacitus is the author of that work because other ancient writers identify him as such.[36] And all the way back in the fourth century, St. Augustine was demonstrating how the same external confirmation of the authors of pagan works confirms the traditional authorship of the New Testament.[37]

In fact, in A.D. 125 the bishop Papias wrote about how he sought knowledge about the apostles from people who had direct contact with them. Concerning the matter of who recorded their teachings he wrote, "Mark, being the recorder of Peter, wrote accurately but not in order whatever he [Peter] remembered of the things either said or done by the Lord. . . . Matthew composed the *logia* [sayings] in Hebrew style; but each recorded them as he was able."[38]

The assumption that the Gospels are anonymous also does not stand up to scrutiny when we compare them to actual anonymous Christian writings. The biblical letter to the Hebrews, for example, *is* anonymous, and in the early Church this manuscript was speculatively attributed to a variety of authors (with Origen of Alexandria saying "only God knows" who wrote it). According to biblical scholar Brant Pitre, "That's what you get with a truly anonymous book of the New Testament: actual anonymous manuscripts, and actual ancient debates over who wrote it. But that's precisely what you *don't* find when it comes to Matthew, Mark, Luke, and John."[39]

Finally, if someone wanted to write fictional literature about Jesus, we would expect him to attribute it to a famous source like St. Peter (which is exactly what happened with the apocryphal Gospel of Peter). But who are Mark and Luke? They're nobodies. It seems more likely, then, that the Gospel of Mark and the Gospel of Luke bear these names simply because these were the authors of those texts. Even the Gospel of Matthew seems unlikely to be a forgery, because although Matthew was an apostle, he had been a tax collector and thus would have been among the lowliest of the apostles.

Granted, the Gospel of John may seem to be a prime candidate for being a forgery because of John's stature, but the fourth Gospel does not explicitly say that John *the apostle* wrote it.[40] If a forger was trying to gain attention for his false Gospel by pretending that John the apostle wrote it, he did a pretty bad job!

. . . The Gospels Are Early and Reliable

What about the claim that the Gospels were written long after the events they purport to describe and so they aren't reliable records of Jesus' ministry? Some ill-informed skeptics claim that the Gospels were written as late as *centuries* after Jesus lived, but even that wouldn't make them completely unreliable.[41] The biographies of Alexander the Great and Siddhartha Gautama (or the Buddha) were written 300-500 years after the death of their subjects, yet most scholars still consider them to be reliable sources about these men.[42]

That said, it's impossible for the Gospels to have been written centuries after Jesus' crucifixion, because by the second century the Church Fathers were already citing them. But even if the Gospels were written as late as A.D. 70–100 (dates typically given by skeptical scholars), that would still be well within a time range for their authors to accurately remember what happened. However, there is evidence the Gospels were written even earlier than these skeptical scholars claim.

Consider that the Acts of the Apostles ends with Paul under house arrest in Rome and does not record his execution in A.D. 64 or the fall of Jerusalem in A.D. 70. Therefore, it is very likely that Acts was written before those events took place. Since Acts is the sequel to the Gospel of Luke, that would place Luke's composition in the early 60s at the latest. And if Mark had been a source for Luke, as most biblical scholars maintain, that would place Mark's Gospel earlier still.

Just as today we have confidence in the ability of Vietnam veterans to remember events that happened decades earlier, we should have confidence that eyewitnesses could accurately remember what happened during Jesus' earthly ministry. In fact, we should have *more* confidence in them, since ancient cultures—lacking computers, printing presses, or even ready paper—were proficient at preserving accurate and detailed oral traditions. Some rabbis could even recite the Torah (the first five books of the Old Testament) from memory!

Furthermore, it's not like the apostles waited to transmit the details of Jesus' life and teachings until they wrote the Gospels decades later. They were traveling preachers who told and re-told these stories in different churches and communities, keeping alive a faithful record of his words and deeds.

The acclaimed Greco-Roman historian A.N. Sherwin-White also tells us that legends cannot corrupt the core historical facts of a narrative that are recorded within two generations of the events it describes.[43] Given that the Gospels were written within this timeframe, he notes how skepticism toward the Gospels is misplaced: "It is astonishing that while Greco-Roman historians have been growing in confidence, the twentieth century study of the Gospel narratives, starting from no less promising material, has taken so gloomy a turn in the development of form criticism."[44]

. . . The Gospels Contain Hints of Historicity

The early Church was sometimes divided by disputes, such as whether it was wrong to eat meat that had been sacrificed to idols (1 Cor. 8). If the early Church had invented the Gospels, we would expect to find Jesus being used in them as a ventriloquist dummy to settle those disputes. But we don't—and this "editorial restraint" supports the view that Gospels are indeed what scholars call *bioi*, or ancient biographies.[45]

However, even if the Gospels were not fabricated but were intended to be authentically biographical, some people may still claim that they're just not *reliable*, because they contradict one another. For example, Ehrman says of the Resurrection accounts, "All four Gospels agree that on the third day after Jesus' crucifixion and burial, Mary Magdalene went to the tomb and found it empty. But on virtually every detail they disagree."[46]

Do these disagreements over details in the most critical part of the Gospels—Jesus' resurrection—undermine their historical reliability? I don't think so, for a few reasons.

First, the Gospels *agree* on the important primary elements of the empty tomb accounts and only vary in secondary details. For example, Mark says the women went to the tomb "when the sun had risen" (Mark 16:2), Matthew says it was "toward the dawn" (Matt. 28:1), Luke says it "early dawn" (Luke 24:1), and John says it was so early it was "still dark" (John 20:1), which all describe the same period around sunrise.

Second, the discrepancy in minor details usually occurs because some details are simply not described, not because there is a blatant contradiction. For example, when John says, "Mary Magdalene came to the tomb early" (John 20:1) he wasn't saying that Mary Magdalene was the *only* woman who went to the tomb (though the Gospels do agree that she was among the several women who went). John was simply focusing on Mary Magdalene and her later response to the disciples.

Third, we don't discount other ancient histories just because of minor discrepancies among them. The Roman historians Suetonius, Dio Cassius, and Tacitus don't agree on where Nero was during the Great Fire of Rome but that doesn't mean Rome didn't burn in A.D. 64.[47] If we trust other ancient accounts in spite of differences in details, why don't we do the same with the Gospels? As the secular historian Michael Grant writes, "[T]he discovery of the empty tomb is differently described by the various Gospels. But if we apply the same sort of criteria that we would apply to any other ancient literary sources, then the evidence is firm and plausible enough to necessitate the conclusion that the tomb was indeed found empty."[48]

Finally, these differences actually count *in favor* of the Gospels' authenticity, because if the Gospels were all strictly identical to one another we would only have one source for Jesus' life, not four, which would be less trustworthy.

Moreover, in some cases these differences subtly harmonize with one another and reveal details that are beyond the creative abilities of any forger.[49] For example, before Jesus miraculously fed 5,000 people he said to Philip, "How are we to buy bread, so that these people may eat?" (John 6:5). Why would Jesus ask Philip, a fairly minor apostle, this important question, instead of someone to whom he had given more authority, like Peter or Andrew?

The answer can be found in Luke's account of the same miracle, which says the feeding of the 5,000 took place outside the town of Bethsaida (Luke 9:10). Peter, Andrew, and Phillip were all from Bethsaida (John 1:44), but Mark tells us that Peter and Andrew were currently living in Capernaum (Mark 1:29). This means that Philip would have been more likely to know who was currently selling goods like bread in the city—because he recently lived there.

Mark's account also tells us that before the feeding of the 5,000, Jesus implored the disciples to come with him to a quiet place because "many were coming and going, and they had no leisure even to eat" (Mark 6:31). Why were so many coming and going? The answer is only found in John's account, which tells us it was Passover (John 6:4). E.P. Sanders, an expert in Judaism during the time of Jesus, estimates that between 300,000 and 500,000 Jews visited Jerusalem during Passover, so we can understand why it was so busy![50]

All of these elements, combined with the advances of scholarly historical studies in recent years, further support the reliability of the Gospels.[51] Peter Kreeft and Ronald Tacelli ably summarize the hopeful attitude we should have to these inspired texts:

> Complex, clever hypothesis after hypothesis follows another with bewildering rapidity and complexity in the desperate attempt to debunk, "demythologize" or demean the data—like declawing a lion. No book in history has been so attacked, cut up, reconstituted, and stood on its head as the New Testament. Yet it still lives—like Christ himself.[52]

COUNTERFEITS
from Atheists

4

Mythical Messiah

In 2012, I debated Jim Travis, a representative from the local chapter of the Freedom from Religion Foundation, on the question, "Does God exist?"[53] In the debate I wanted to show that God is not just the ultimate cause of the universe, but that he also loves us and wants to save us from our sins. That's why I provided evidence for the one miracle that proves the veracity of Christianity: Jesus' bodily resurrection from the dead.

In response to this evidence, Travis claimed I had actually provided "no proof" for my case and dismissed any evidence I offered from the Bible. During cross-examination I asked Travis a question that exposed his radical skepticism:

"Well, do you believe Jesus even existed?"

"No I don't," he replied in a mater-of-fact tone. "There were many historians, many who lived at that time and none of them wrote about Jesus. There are many historians who don't think there ever was a Jesus."

Now there's a counterfeit Christ—one that simply never existed.

But how can that be true if . . .
. . . Most Ancient Historians Wouldn't Have Cared

When Jim said, "There are many historians who say Jesus never existed," I asked an obvious follow-up question.

"What historians?"

Jim simply repeated, "Many historians!" which elicited a healthy amount of laughter from the audience. But according to Bart Ehrman, "The view that Jesus existed is held by virtually every expert on the planet."[54] Jim was probably referring to popular writers (almost all of whom are not historians or New Testament scholars) who claim that an absence of ancient testimony about Jesus proves he never existed.

For example, in their book the *Jesus Mysteries*, Timothy Freke and Peter Gandy list twenty-four ancient authors who lived within 100 years of Jesus, and wonder why none of them describe Jesus' life or miracles.[55] This style of argument actually goes back to a 1909 list devised by the skeptic John Remsburg that includes:

> Philo-Judaeus, Seneca, Pliny the Elder, Juvenal, Martial, Persius, Plutarch, Justus of Tiberius, Apollonius, Quintilian, Lucanus, Epictetus, Silius Italicus, Statius, Ptolemy, Hermogones, Valerius Maximus, Arrian, Petronius, Dion Pruseus, Paterculus, Appian, Theon of Smyrna, Phlegon, Pompon Mela, Quintius Curtius, Lucian, Pausanias, Valerius Flaccus, Florus Lucius, Favorinus, Phaedrus, Damis, Aulus Gellius, Columella, Dio Chrysostom, Lysias, Appion of Alexandria.

But these lists are flawed, because they assume these authors (if they even knew who Jesus was) would have *wanted* to write about Jesus.

For starters, many of these authors didn't even write about history. Pausanias and Pompon Mela wrote Greek and Roman geographies. Ptolemy and Pliny the Elder were scientists who recorded information about the natural world. Theon of Smyrna, Favorinus, and Gellius wrote reflections on philosophy (Theon's only surviving work is entitled *On Mathematics Useful for the Understanding of Plato*). Other writers, such as Hermogenes, Quintilian, Apollonius Dyscolus, and Dio Chrysostom focused on practical subjects like speechmaking. And Columella limited his writing to the subject of trees that existed within the Roman Empire!

Moreover, many of the authors who *were* historians did not usually write about the time period in which Jesus lived. Statius, Flaccus, and Apollonius the Sophist only wrote about ancient Greek subjects, and Arrian is best known for his chronicles about Alexander the Great—who lived 400 years before Christ. Many of these authors didn't even write about *Christians*, but that doesn't prove there were no Christians in the first and second century. (There were; we have their writings.)

But wouldn't some of these authors have "taken a break" from their normal subjects in order to write about someone who performed incredible miracles like Jesus? Well, if they did hear these accounts, they probably would have dismissed them as idle tales about a failed messiah. Historian John Meier puts it well: "Jesus was a marginal Jew leading a marginal movement in a marginal province of a vast Roman Empire. The wonder is that any learned Jew or pagan would have known or referred to him at all in the first or early second century."[56]

The few non-biblical sources that do attest to Jesus only mention him because of the surprising fact that his followers did not abandon this "marginal Jew."

. . . Some Ancient Historians *Did* Write About Jesus

The Roman historian Tacitus records in his *Annals* that after the great fire in Rome, Emperor Nero fastened the blame on a despised group of people called Christians. Tacitus identifies this group thusly: "Christus, the founder of the name, was put to death by Pontius Pilate, procurator of Judea in the reign of Tiberius." Biblical scholar F.F. Bruce says, "It may be regarded as an instance of the irony of history that the only surviving reference to [Pontius Pilate] in a pagan writer mentions him because of the sentence of death which he passed on Christ."[57]

Some critics object that Tacitus only speaks of *Christ*, which is a title that does not specifically refer to Jesus by name. But the reason Tacitus does this is in order to show his readers that Christ was the founder of a new and popularly despised religion named after him. Connecting the title of *Christ* to Christians without explaining the word's meaning is like saying Buddhists follow a man named Buddha, even though Buddha is not a name but a title that means "enlightened one."

Most scholars agree that this passage is genuine, not a later Christian addition to the text. If it were an interpolation, we would expect blame for Jesus' death to be placed on the Jewish leaders, rather than Pilate, so as not to incur the wrath of Roman officials who were persecuting the Church. According to James Rives, a classical scholar who has edited a book on Tacitus, "I've never come across any dispute about the authenticity of *Annals*. 15.44; as far as I'm aware, it's always been accepted as genuine."[58]

Along with Tacitus, the first-century Jewish historian Josephus mentions Jesus twice. The longer passage is called the *Testimonium Flavianum*. Scholars are divided on this passage because, although it does mention Jesus, it contains phrases that later Christian copyists almost certainly added. These

include phrases that would never have been used by an unconverted Jew like Josephus, such as, "He was the Christ"
and, "He appeared alive again on the third day."

According to New Testament scholar James D.G. Dunn,
the passage has clearly been subject to Christian additions,
but there are also words in it that Christians would never
use. These include calling Jesus "a wise man" or referring to
themselves as a "tribe"—which is strong evidence Josephus
originally wrote something very close to the following:

> At this time there appeared Jesus, a wise man. For he was
> a doer of startling deeds, a teacher of people who received
> the truth with pleasure. And he gained a following both
> among many Jews and among many of Greek origin. And
> when Pilate, because of an accusation made by the lead-
> ing men among us, condemned him to the cross, those
> who had loved him previously did not cease to do so. And
> up until this very day the tribe of Christians (named after
> him) has not died out.[59]

In the second, shorter reference, Josephus describes the
stoning of lawbreakers in A.D. 62. One of the criminals is described as "the brother of Jesus, who was called Christ, whose
name was James." What makes this passage authentic is that it
lacks Christian terms like "the Lord," it fits into the context
of this section of Josephus, and it's found in every manuscript
copy of the *Antiquities*. According to New Testament scholar
Robert Van Voorst, "The overwhelming majority of scholars
hold that the words 'brother of Jesus, who was called Christ,'
are authentic, as is the entire passage in which it is found."[60]

Finally, it is prejudicial not to include the authors of the
New Testament among the list of "ancient witnesses" who attest to the existence of Jesus, especially when their testimony

contradicts the mythicist thesis. That's because the simplest argument against mythicism is this: how did Christianity begin without a founder like Jesus of Nazareth who inspired and commissioned the apostles?

Mythicists answer this argument by claiming that Christianity began with a few people, like Peter and Paul, who had hallucinatory visions of a heavenly Jesus. Over the next few decades these stories turned into legends about an earthly Jesus.

But the *earliest* sources we have about Jesus—the writings of St. Paul—describe Jesus having an earthly existence. Paul makes it clear Jesus was a man who was descended from David (Rom. 1:1–3), was born of a woman (Gal. 4:4), had a last supper with his disciples (1 Cor. 11:23–26), and was crucified and rose from the dead (1 Cor. 15:3–7).

Some critics object that this isn't enough, because Paul doesn't mention specific events and miracles that took place during Jesus' ministry. But early Christians who wrote long after the Gospels were composed also did not describe key parts of Jesus' ministry. The Acts of the Apostles, the letters of John, the book of Revelation, as well as non-biblical texts like 1 Clement, the letter of Barnabas, and the letters of Ignatius, all emphasize Jesus' death and resurrection but do not describe major aspects of his earthly ministry.

Since Christians who knew the Gospel stories felt free not to mention them in their writings about Jesus, we cannot conclude Paul was unaware of those stories just because he didn't mention them, either.

. . . The First Christians Believed in an Earthly Jesus

Paul's connection to the historical Jesus is verified when he tells us about people who were "in Christ before him" who gave him information about Jesus. In Galatians 1:18–19,

Paul even says he knew the apostles and writes, "After three years I went up to Jerusalem to visit Cephas, and remained with him fifteen days. But I saw none of the other apostles except James the Lord's brother." As the famous New Testament scholar C.H. Dodd once said, "We may presume they did not spend all that time talking about the weather."[61]

Instead, Paul was able to use those two weeks to corroborate what Jesus revealed to him (Acts 9:3–6, Gal. 1:16) with what Jesus had taught to the apostles—including one apostle named James who was one of Jesus' relatives (in Greek, the word for *brother* can also mean cousin or step-brother). If Jesus had a relative that Paul communicated with, he could not possibly have been a myth.

This is why mythicists have to say that Paul meant that James was only a spiritual "brother" of the Lord—just as today Christians will call one another "brother" and "sister." But when Paul identifies someone as being a Christian or "brother in the Lord," he just calls him "the brother" like he does for Quartus in Romans 16:23 or Apollos in 1 Corinthians 16:12.[62] The term "brother of the Lord" must therefore have a meaning beyond simply being a Christian. According to Bart Ehrman:

> When [Paul] says that along with Cephas [Peter], the only apostle he saw was "James, the brother of the Lord," he could not mean the terms brother in a loose generic sense to mean "believer." Cephas was also a believer, and so were the other apostles. And so he must mean it in the specific sense.[63]

Moreover, if Jesus were a myth then the Gospels would have to be completely mythical as well. That's why Richard Carrier believes that Mark wrote a meta-parable derived from the Old Testament rather than a kind of ancient biography. But what makes this thesis strange is that we know of no "meta-parables" as long as the Gospels in the entire Greco-Roman world. Moreover, if Mark's entire Gospel were an allegory, all the incidental historical details in it couldn't be incidental or historical: they'd have to have a deeper allegorical meaning.

For example, in Mark 15:21 we read that Simon of Cyrene was forced to carry Jesus' cross and that he happened to be the father of Alexander and Rufus. The traditional interpretation of this passage is that Mark's Roman audience probably knew of Alexander and Rufus and that's why Mark included this detail. In Romans 16:13, Paul even sends greetings to a Rufus, who was "eminent in the Lord." But if these two people existed and their father knew Jesus, then the mythicist theory fails.

Carrier, therefore, says this reference is part of an allegory wherein Simon of Cyrene represents Cyreanean hedonistic philosophy. This philosophy gave birth to Alexander, who represents the failed military ideals of Alexander the Great, as well as Rufus, who represents the first-century cynic philosophy of Gaius Musonius Rufus. Jesus' contact with Simon represents how the celestial Christ nullified the worldly passions of the Cyreanean philosophers.

Or, as Carrier puts it, "The way of Cyrene (attachment to the world) gave birth to the two ways of the world (military might and man-made philosophy), which end in destruction—unless we submit to God. Those worldly ways were just what Christ had destroyed along with his own flesh."[64]

What can we say to this? Well, just as when we hear hoof beats in the distance we should think *horses* and not *unicorns*, when we see incidental historical details in the Gospels it makes much more sense to treat them as such and not read complex allegories into them when the evidence does not warrant it.

Finally, if the mythicist theory were true, then at some point in Christian history there would have been a break or outright conflict between new converts who believed in a real Jesus and the older establishment view that Jesus never existed. The early Christian leaders, known as Church Fathers, loved to stamp out heresy. They wrote massive treatises criticizing heretics and erroneous ideas about Jesus—and yet in all of their writings, the heresy that Jesus never existed is never mentioned.

Amazingly, no one in the *entire history of Christianity* (not even early pagan critics like Celsus or Lucian) seriously argued for a mythical Jesus until the eighteenth century.[65] Alternate theories about Christianity plagued the Church for century after century, yet mythicism is never among them. This makes it likely that Christians always believed in a historical Jesus, because such a person really did exist.

5

Pagan Copycat

One night during college, in between playing video games and drinking more soda than any human being should ingest, my friend Will and I started to talk about my conversion to Catholicism. As the clock ticked past midnight, he went over to his computer and said, "Dude, you've got to see this documentary. It will change *everything* you think about religion."

I pulled up a chair and he clicked on a video called *Zeitgeist*. The cover showed the earth with a steel cage wrapped around it and the trailer ominously warned that "there are people guiding your life and you don't even know it."

"Come on man, you don't really buy into this stuff, do you?" I said.

"Just hear them out!" he pleaded.

I only made it through a third of the movie, but it was the part that Will wanted me to see—because it claimed Jesus never existed. But rather than claiming that Jesus' later followers mixed up fact with legend, the movie said that stories about Jesus were copied from pagan mythology. Whether Egyptian, Greek, or Persian, it said, in all these ancient religions there were gods who happened to be born of a virgin on December 25, were accompanied by twelve disciples, performed miracles, were crucified, and then rose from the dead.

Don't think for a second that such theories are only found among a fringe group of people on the internet. *Zeitgeist* has viewed millions of times in Youtube alone, and there are dozens of books and articles out there claiming that the story of Jesus is just a mish-mash of older pagan savior myths.

"How do you explain all that?" Will asked. "I mean it's basically the same story, ripped off from other places!"

But how can that be true if . . .
. . . The Parallels Are Strained or Nonexistent

In 1961, Samuel Sandmel published an article in the *Journal of the Society of Biblical Literature* that described the phenomena of *parallelomania*. This happens when scholars try to find any similarities between two stories, no matter how strained, and then claim that these "parallels" *prove* one of the sources is copying the other.

A prime example of this is Joseph Atwill's 2005 book, *Caesar's Messiah: The Roman Conspiracy to Invent Jesus*. He claims there are parallels between the writings of Josephus and the Gospels showing that the latter are just fictionalized accounts of the former. Atwill makes other fringe thinkers look mainstream, as he claims that not only did Jesus not exist, but neither did Peter, James, the other apostles, or even St. Paul.

For example, Atwill says that when Jesus called the disciples to be "fishers of men" (Matt. 4:19) this is a coded reference to a scene in Josephus's *Jewish War* where Jews try to escape murderous Romans by swimming in the Sea of Galilee. In other words, the call to evangelize is really an ironic reference to when the Romans "caught Jews like fish" in the

Battle of Lake Tiberias.[66] This is such a textbook example of parallelomania that even Atwill's mythicist colleagues like Robert Price have rebuked his work.[67]

But the alleged parallels between Jesus and other pagan deities in *Zeitgeist* are just as implausible. For example, *Zeitgeist* says, "Mithra, of Persia, born of a virgin on December 25; he had twelve disciples and performed miracles, and upon his death was buried for three days and thus resurrected."

Sounds impressive, but is any of it true?

First, the mythical Mithra was *not* born of a virgin. He emerged fully grown from a rock (which is only a "virgin" in the most strained sense of that word).[68] There also isn't any evidence Mithra was born on December 25. That's just made up. Even if he was, the Bible never says Jesus was born on that day; the early Church chose it among several other candidates in order to celebrate Jesus' birth, not to define when it happened.

There *is* a painting of Mithra standing next to twelve figures, but there is no evidence they are disciples (they were probably just references to the Zodiac). There is also no ancient record of Mithra dying or being resurrected from the dead.[69]

When it comes to the Egyptian God Horus, *Zeitgeist* claims:

"[He] was born on December 25 of the virgin Isis-Meri . . . at the age of thirty he was baptized by a figure known as Anup and thus began his ministry. Horus had twelve disciples he traveled about with, performing miracles such as healing the sick and walking on water. . . . Horus was crucified, buried for three days, and thus, resurrected."

Most of the Jesus/Horus connection comes from the bad scholarship of nineteenth-century amateur Egyptologists like Gerald Massey and Alvin Boyd Kuhn. Tom Harpur writes in his book *The Pagan Christ* (which is dedicated to Kuhn) that "there was a Jesus in Egyptian lore many thousands of years ago." His name was Iusu, Iusa, according to Gerald Massey, and that name means "the coming divine Son who heals or saves."[70]

But according to Egyptologist Ron Leprohon, they "have the syntax all wrong. In any event, the name 'Isua' simply does not exist in Egyptian."[71] The standard etymology of the name *Jesus* comes from the Hebrew word for Joshua (*Yehoshu'a*), which means "Yahweh is salvation."

There is also no evidence among ancient Egyptian records that Anup baptized Horus or that Horus had twelve disciples. Horus's conception occurred when his mother Isis engaged in sexual relations with the dead body of his father Osiris (hardly a "virgin birth").[72] The claim that Horus was crucified is based solely on images of Horus standing with his arms spread wide. The standard account of his death describes Horus being bitten or stung by a scorpion and his grieving mother asking the God Thoth to bring him back to life.[73]

Indeed, many of the so-called resurrections in ancient mythology are just reanimations of the deceased, which are far different from Jesus' glorious resurrection to immortal life. This includes Horus's own father Osiris, whose dead body was dismembered and scattered around Egypt before being re-assembled to allow Osiris to become the undead ruler of the underworld.[74]

The parallels between Jesus and Greco-Roman deities fare no better, like *Zeitgeist's* claim that "Dionysus of Greece, born of a virgin on December 25, was a traveling teacher who performed miracles such as turning water into wine."

Although Dionysus was a Greek god of wine and festivals, he is never said to have turned water into wine as Jesus did at the wedding of Cana. Instead, in one story he replaced the water in a spring with wine that tasted like water (so that he could rape a water nymph). According to New Testament scholar Carsten Claussen, "None of the scant supposed parallels from Hellenistic sources displays a changing of water into wine. The parallels are not close enough to explain the origin of the tradition behind John 2:1–11."[75]

There is also no source before the time of Christ that identifies Dionysus' birthday as December 25. Dionysus has a complicated birth story that involves him being conceived after Zeus had physical relations with women like Persephone or Demeter. These are not "virgin births," because the women have physical relations with gods that have human forms. These encounters are not like the Holy Spirit "overshadowing" Mary in a way that precludes her having intercourse with anyone, divine or human (Luke 1:35).

Finally, the Greek god Attis was not, as *Zeitgeist* claims, "born of a virgin" but, in most accounts, came into existence when blood or divine bodily fluids spilled on the ground. This caused a tree to grow whose fruit later impregnates a human woman. Attis was not crucified but died under a tree and, according to Giulia Gasparro, "The notion of a 'resurrection' of Attis does not belong to the Phrygian mythical-ritual context."[76]

These claims about Attis probably have their origin in an 1875 book by Kersey Graves called *The World's Sixteen Crucified Saviors*. In one of its chapters there is a header that reads "Atys of Phrygia Crucified 1170 B.C." Graves then writes of Attis, without evidence, "He was suspended on a tree, crucified, buried, and rose again."[77] But this book is so inaccurate that one prominent atheist website lists a warning saying that "readers should be extremely cautious in trusting *anything* [emphasis in the original] in this book."[78]

. . . The Plausible Parallels Are Too Late

Sometimes the parallels between Jesus and a pagan source are real and uncannily close, but that's only because the pagan source is *copying the story of Jesus.*

In Mithraism, for example, there is a communal meal that Justin Martyr says was an imitation of the Christian Eucharist.[79] According to Mithraic scholar Richard Gordon, the Roman Mithra cult began no earlier than the early second century, so there's no way it could have influenced the New Testament documents that were written decades earlier.[80] Another Mithraic scholar also informs us that "Justin is comparing only the *ceremony.* . . . It would be quite wrong to say that he is comparing the Mithraic *theology* with the Christian one that the bread and cup 'represent' the body and blood of Christ [emphasis in the original]."[81] So not only did the Christian part of the parallel come first, it's not even a substantive parallel.

Even scholars who should know better succumb to this kind of error. For example, in the first pages of his book *How Jesus Became God,* Bart Ehrman tells a story about a first-century miracle worker believed to be the Son of God who survived his own death. But instead of Jesus, Ehrman reveals he's talking about a contemporary of Jesus named Apollonius of Tyana. This sets the stage for Ehrman to talk about how ancient stories about men becoming gods were common and so the Jesus story should be regarded as a similar kind of folklore.[82]

Less sophisticated critics appeal to the Apollonius story as another "pagan influence" behind the story of Christ without noting it was first told by a Greek writer named Philostratus in the third century *after* Christ was born. Ehrman himself neglects to mention that Philostratus is our only source for the life of Apollonius and that the wife of Emperor Septimius Severus (A.D. 145–211) commissioned him to write a biography about Apollonius.[83] Maria Dzielska notes that the Apollonius legend grew "thanks to a governor of Bithynia— Sossianus Hierocles, who used Philostratus's work, none too popular in the third century, to combat Christianity."[84]

Ehrman acknowledges this theory in a footnote, but then claims that all he is doing is showing how belief in "God-men" was easily accepted in the Roman cultural context. But if belief in a God-man like Apollonius was only easily accepted because it was crafted to *imitate Jesus*, that still doesn't explain how belief in Jesus' divinity came about among fiercely monotheistic first-century Jews. The Jewish philosopher Philo tells us that the Jews in Jerusalem rioted against Pontius Pilate simply because of golden shields he erected in Jerusalem that bore an *inscription* saying Emperor Tiberius was the Son of God.[85] Why would these same devout believers completely abandon Jewish monotheism in favor of a pagan savior myth?

The answer is, "They wouldn't," and as T.N.D. Mettinger observes in his scholarly monograph *Riddle of the Resurrection: Dying and Rising Gods in the Ancient Near East*:

> There is, as far as I am aware, no *prima facie* evidence that the death and resurrection of Jesus is a mythological construct, drawing on myths and rites of the dying and rising gods of the surrounding world. While studied with profit against the background of Jewish resurrection belief, the faith in the death and resurrection of Jesus retains its unique character in the history of religions.[86]

The biggest problem with the "pagan copycat" thesis is that it assumes the first followers of Jesus came to believe in his resurrection simply because they heard stories about resurrections in other pagan mythologies. But ancient Jews knew these pagan stories were just that—stories.

More importantly, Jesus' resurrection was not like any of those stories. It was not an assumption into heaven like what was claimed for other mythological god-men (what is called *apotheosis*). It also was not an ahistorical, mythical-poetical idea like that of pagan deities who "die" every winter and are "reborn" every spring in unison with the crop cycle. Ehrman even admits that, apart from Apollonius of Tyana, "I don't know of any other cases in ancient Greek or Roman thought of this kind of 'God-man,' where an already existing divine being is said to be born of a mortal woman."[87]

If the third-century account of Apollonius is derived from the story of Jesus, that makes the story of the "God-man" Jesus all the more exceptional and difficult to explain—apart from the Incarnation actually taking place.

Gerd Ludemann is a scholar who denies that Jesus rose from the dead, but even he affirms that the apostles had *some* sort of experience of the risen Christ. The claim that Jesus appeared to his disciples shortly after his death could not be a later legend. Ludemann writes, "It may be taken as historically certain that Peter and the disciples had experiences after Jesus' death in which Jesus appeared to them as the risen Christ."[88] The question we must ask is, "What explains these appearances?"

Ludemann and many skeptical scholars believe that the apostles simply had grief-induced hallucinations. Is this explanation sufficient to explain the unique and verifiable historical facts associated with Jesus' bodily resurrection from the dead?

Rotting Corpse

Sit and smile. That was all I could do, even though I wanted to rebut my debate opponent Dan Barker during his closing speech. Dan was once a Protestant pastor, but ever since his "de-conversion" in the 1980s he has become a kind of preacher for atheism (he currently serves as the co-president of the Freedom From Religion Foundation). In 2015 we debated whether or not God existed, and three years later we were on stage at Minnesota State University to debate a more specific question: "Does the Christian God exist?"[89]

I thought the debate went well. I was able to neutralize Dan's tactic of scattering dozens of difficult Bible verses in an effort to make the God of the Bible look like a moral monster. By the time we got to cross-examination, I was prepared to dive into one argument Dan had not addressed yet: my evidence for Jesus' resurrection.

But instead of addressing the evidence I raised, Dan just went right back to the alleged atrocities of the Old Testament. It was only during his closing statement, which was the last speech of the night, that Dan addressed my arguments. He claimed that what really happened after Good Friday was that the apostles believed Jesus' *spirit* rose from the dead while his body still lay in the tomb. For them, that was enough to turn defeat into victory; yet modern Christians have misunderstood their theology ever since.

But how can that be true if . . .
. . . St. Paul Believed in a Bodily Resurrection

It's bad form to bring up new arguments or objections in your closing statement because your opponent has no opportunity to respond to them. I was frustrated, but I held my tongue. I didn't get the chance that night to rebut Dan's "spiritual resurrection" hypothesis. But now I *do* have the chance—so here's what's wrong with it.

First, the earliest testimony we have about the Resurrection comes from St. Paul's letters, which describe Jesus undergoing a bodily resurrection from the dead. Dan tries to get around this fact by claiming that Paul used a Greek word for Jesus' resurrection that only refers to spiritual resurrection. Specifically, *egeiro,* which just means "rise" or "wake up." He does not use the word that means "resurrection" (*anastasis, anistemi*). Barker also claims:

> It is perfectly consistent with Christian theology to think that the spirit of Jesus, not his body, was awakened from the grave, as Christians today believe that the spirit of Grandpa has gone to heaven while his body rots in the ground. In fact, just a few verses later Paul confirms this: 'Flesh and blood cannot inherit the kingdom of God.' The physical body is not important to Christian theology.[90]

Yet in Romans 1:4, Paul says that Jesus was "designated Son of God in power according to the Spirit of holiness by his resurrection [*anastaseos*] from the dead." Contra Barker,

Paul *does* describe Jesus rising from the dead with a form of the Greek word *anastasis*. Moreover, in 1 Corinthians 15 Paul uses *egeiro* and *anastasis* interchangeably when speaking about the relationship between our future resurrection from the dead and Christ's resurrection. Paul writes:

> Now if Christ is preached as raised [*egegertai*] from the dead, how can some of you say that there is no resurrection [*anastasis*] of the dead? But if there is no resurrection [*anastasis*] of the dead, then Christ has not been raised [*egegertai*]. If Christ has not been raised [*egegertai*], then our preaching is in vain and your faith is in vain (1 Cor. 15:12–14).

Paul's argument is simple: if we don't rise from the dead, then Christ didn't rise from the dead. But since Christ did rise from the dead we can be confident that we too will rise from the dead.

What about Barker's citation of 1 Corinthians 15:50 ("Flesh and blood cannot inherit the kingdom of God") and Paul's general use of the term "spiritual body"? Well, we have to remember what Paul was up against in Corinth.

Pauline scholar John Ziesler believes that Paul was trying to convince people that the resurrection of the dead is not a mere reanimation of one's corpse. For Paul, the "spiritual body" in the Resurrection "seems to mean something like 'outward form,' or 'embodiment' or perhaps better 'the way in which the person is conveyed and expressed' . . . a resurrection of the whole person, involving embodiment but not physical embodiment."[91]

When Paul writes, "Flesh and blood cannot inherit the kingdom of God," he is using a Semitism—a Jewish way of speaking—about the natural state of humanity apart from the grace of God. We can't inherit the kingdom of God without being moved by God's spirit. However, that doesn't mean that in this kingdom we will only be spirits. *Spiritual*, in this context, refers to a thing's *orientation* as opposed to its *substance*. It's like when we say the Bible is a "spiritual book" or when Paul writes, "The spiritual man judges all things, but is himself to be judged by no one" (1 Cor. 2:15).

The subjects in these statements are not non-physical, ghostly apparitions but books and people ordered toward the will of God. As St. Augustine said, "As the Spirit, when it serves the flesh, is not improperly said to be carnal, so the flesh, when it serves the spirit, will rightly be called spiritual—not because it is changed into spirit, as some suppose who misinterpret the text."[92]

. . . The New Testament Records Jesus' Bodily Appearances

Barker also claims Paul cannot be talking about a bodily resurrection because he describes Jesus "appearing" to the disciples in 1 Corinthians 15. Barker writes that "the word 'appeared' in this passage is also ambiguous and does not require a physical presence. The word *ophthe*, from the verb *horao*, is used for both physical sight as well as spiritual visions."[93] Barker then gives two examples to prove that Paul is talking about the disciples having a purely spiritual vision of Jesus.

The first involves Luke's description of how a man from Macedonia appeared (*opthe*) to Paul in a vision (Acts 16:9–10). The second involves the "appearances" of Moses and Elijah on the Mount of Transfiguration (Matt. 17:3). Barker asks the reader, "Did Moses and Elijah appear physically to Peter? Shall we start looking for their empty tombs? This is obviously some kind of visionary appearance."[94]

But Barker's argument doesn't work because a person can "appear" to someone without being a ghost or spirit. I can ask my wife, "Are you going to make an appearance at our party tonight?" without expecting her to materialize out of thin air. In the incident with the Macedonian, Luke makes it clear he's talking about a *dream* Paul had—"a vision appeared to Paul in the night" (Acts 16:9). But when Paul and the other New Testament authors talk about Jesus appearing to the disciples, they don't describe those appearances as being part of a vision or dream.

For example, Luke describes the disciples saying, "The Lord has risen indeed, and has appeared to Simon!" (Luke 24:34). Luke uses the word *opthe* to describe this appearance, but in the proceeding verses he records Jesus appearing in an explicitly embodied form. Jesus tells the apostles, "See my hands and my feet, that it is I myself; handle me, and see; for a spirit has not flesh and bones as you see that I have" (Luke 24:39).

Barker's use of Moses' and Elijah's appearing on the Mount of Transfiguration backfires, because the text does not describe a purely visionary experience. 2 Kings 2:11 tells us that Elijah went up alive into heaven and Jude 9 alludes to a Jewish legend about Moses' body being taken up to heaven. It would be entirely appropriate that these men appeared to Peter with bodies that God protected from death and decay. Peter even declares that he will build a tent for Moses and Elijah (Matt. 17:4), and no one present corrects Peter's suggestion by saying that it is only the *spirits* of Moses and Elijah that are present and so tents are unnecessary.

Finally, Paul was a Pharisee, so he believed in a future, bodily resurrection. But unlike the unconverted Pharisees, Paul taught that our bodies will be transformed so that they resemble Jesus' glorified resurrection body. He told the Philippians, "We await a Savior, the Lord Jesus Christ, who will change our lowly body to be like his glorious body" (3:20–21). To the Church at Rome he wrote, "If the Spirit of him who raised Jesus from the dead dwells in you, he who raised Christ Jesus from the dead will give life to your mortal bodies also through his Spirit who dwells in you" (8:11).

This expectation would not make sense unless the first Christians believed that Jesus' body was gloriously reigning in heaven rather than rotting away in a tomb outside of Jerusalem.

. . . The Hallucination Hypothesis Can't Explain Everything

In his debates and books, Barker uses a variant of the *hallucination hypothesis* to explain the post-resurrection appearances of Jesus to his disciples. He claims that Peter felt so guilty after denying Jesus at his trial that he imagined he heard the voice of Jesus consoling him after the Crucifixion. Barker conjectures that after hearing such a voice, "Peter triumphantly tells his friends, 'I talked with Jesus! He is not dead! I am forgiven!' His friends say, 'Peter talked with Jesus? Peter met Jesus? He's alive! It's a *spiritual* kingdom!'"[95]

One problem with this idea is that hallucinations of a risen Jesus do not explain the datum of Jesus' empty tomb. In my book *Why We're Catholic,* I presented several pieces of evidence for the historicity of Jesus' empty tomb, including its verifiable location in Jerusalem and the testimony of the Church's enemies who indirectly acknowledged it was empty by claiming that the disciples stole Jesus' body.[96]

Another piece is the fact that *women* were said to have discovered the tomb. Even in the second century, critics of the Church were using this detail to attack the Resurrection accounts. In his dispute with Origen, for instance, the pagan writer Celsus mocked Origen for trusting the testimony of a "half-frantic woman."[97] Luke tells us that the men even checked the tomb for themselves in order to verify what the women said about it (Luke 24:11–12).

If the discovery of Jesus' empty tomb had been a fabrication, we would expect the Gospel's authors to have grounded this detail in more reliable characters—like the male apostles or even the Jewish and Roman officials. Since they didn't, this makes it more likely the account is historical and wasn't invented to support belief in the Resurrection.

In our debate, though, Barker dismissed this detail. Women were always associated with tombs, he said, because they anointed the bodies of the deceased. Therefore, we would expect a detail like this even in a completely fabricated account of the Resurrection. But that doesn't explain why a fabricated account of the empty tomb would *rely* on female testimony—even if it did include it.

The Evangelists could have, for example, depicted the men going with the women in order to roll away the stone (in Mark 16:3, the women even ask themselves, "Who will roll away the stone for us from the door of the tomb?"). In the later, apocryphal Gospel of Peter, Jesus emerges from the tomb in the presence of both the Jewish elders and the Roman guards (one of whom is named Petronius). But this account still includes the details about the women visiting the tomb because, as one scholar notes, "it was so much a part of the Easter story that the redactor could not leave it out."[98]

Furthermore, as N.T. Wright points out in his book *The Resurrection of the Son of God,* there are no examples in the pagan world or in Jewish thought of belief in a person dying, experiencing the afterlife, and then returning to a glorified, immortal, bodily existence in the present life. If the apostles had somehow all hallucinated the same thing, they would have imagined something familiar to them—like a Christ who had been spiritually assumed into heaven. But as we've seen, they preached that Jesus experienced a *bodily* resurrection from the dead, which Jews of the time did not believe could happen until the end of the world.

Finally, we should be skeptical of the idea that the apostles experienced grief-induced group hallucinations of any kind. Instead of this exceedingly rare phenomenon, it would have been more likely for them simply to do what followers of other messiah figures, like Theudas or "the Egyptian,"[99] did. Rather than hallucinate that these men had risen from the dead (either spiritually or physically), many simply gave up on the idea of a Messiah and returned to their regular lives. Others went on, as Wright puts it, to find a "new Messiah"—even within the deceased's family.

But the followers of Jesus did not do either of these things, which leads Wright to ask:

> Why did Christianity even begin, let alone continue, as a messianic movement, when its Messiah so obviously not only did not do what a Messiah was supposed to do but suffered a fate which ought to have showed conclusively that he could not possibly have been Israel's anointed? . . . Their answer, consistently throughout the evidence we possess, was that Jesus, following his execution on a charge of being a would-be Messiah, had been raised from the dead.[100]

COUNTERFEITS
from Non-Christians

Rabbi Yeshua

One night, while I was staying with a host family on a mission trip, my hosts asked my teammate John and me about our faiths. John was Protestant and was never at a loss for words in a conversation (which I appreciated at the end of a long day when I wanted a break from talking). But as he began to answer, one of the hosts interrupted John and said, "I think we've heard enough from you." She then turned to me: "What about you? What's your religious background?"

"Oh, I'm Catholic. Well, my Dad is Jewish and my mom used to be Catholic, but I came into the Catholic Church about ten years ago."

The wife was delighted, because she was also Catholic, but her husband didn't seem amused. Later I learned that he was Jewish and the couple had an interfaith marriage. As we left the next morning, the husband gave me a wry smile and said, "I'll have to send you some books on Judaism, you little turncoat."

Though he meant it in jest, the issue of Jews becoming Christians is a sensitive one in the Jewish community; feelings of "betrayal" are not an infrequent reaction to news that someone has converted.[101] Ancient and medieval Jewish writers described Jesus as having been born of an affair Mary had with a Roman soldier named Pantera, which is a pun derived from the similarity between the name *Panthera* and the Greek word for virgin, *parthenos*. They describe Jesus as an evil sorcerer who used the power of Yahweh's name to perform miracles and subsequently led people away from worshipping him.[102]

Modern Jews have adopted a much more positive view of Jesus, and tend to blame his immediate followers for the tensions that have arisen between Jews and Christians since the first century. According to Rabbi Shmuley Boteach:

> Once Jesus is stripped of his anti-Semitic cloak and re-stored as the wise rabbi and devoted Jewish patriot he was, there is much Jews can learn from him. But the Jews have not and cannot ever accept Jesus as he exists in Christian theology . . . belief in a messiah who did not fulfill the messianic prophecies is anathema to us Jews, a fact that will never change.[103]

From the modern Jewish perspective, Jesus was a misunderstood rabbi who taught people to follow the Torah and never claimed to be either the Messiah or God incarnate. After his death, Jesus' followers twisted the Hebrew Bible's prophecies to fit his life and then turned against their Jewish brethren by couching Jesus' teachings in anti-Semitic descriptions of Jews who did not become Christians.

But how can that be true if . . .
. . . The New Testament Is Not Anti-Semitic

One Jewish objection to Jesus is that he could not have inspired the authors of the New Testament because the New Testament promotes hatred of Jews. Jesus must instead be a rabbi whom the first Christians misunderstood, heaping blame and scorn on "the Jews" who persecuted their Lord (John 7:1).

Because half of my family is Jewish I'm more sensitive than many people to the presence of anti-Semitism, including how even a term like "the Jews" can have anti-Semitic undertones. But the authors of the New Testament were faithful Jews (except for the Gentile Luke) that followed a Messiah who was "born under the law" (Gal. 4:4).

In the first century, debate about Jesus' messianic identity was debate *between Jews,* and rival Jewish schools often used very harsh language with one another. Evidence from the Dead Sea Scrolls shows that they would call their fellow Jews "sons of darkness," "sons of the pit," and tools of Satan! Craig Evans says:

> The polemic found in the writings of Qumran [where the Dead Sea Scrolls were found] surpasses in intensity that of the New Testament. In contrast to Qumran's esoteric and exclusive posture, the early Church proclaimed its message and invited all believers to join its fellowship. Never does the New Testament enjoin Christians to curse unbelievers or opponents. Never does the New Testament petition God to damn the enemies of the Church. But Qumran did.[104]

When John talks about "the Jews" (Greek: *hoi Ioudaioi*) he's talking about specific Jewish leaders in Jerusalem, not every Jew at that time. One example that makes this clear involves the aftermath of Jesus' healing of the man who had been blind since birth. John tells us, "The Jews did not believe that he had been blind and had received his sight, until they called the parents of the man who had received his sight" (John 9:18).

They told them that their son was an adult and they could ask him directly about the matter. John then reveals, "His parents said this because they feared the Jews, for the Jews had already agreed that if anyone should confess him to be Christ, he was to be put out of the synagogue" (John 9:22).

But this man's parents were *Jewish,* so "the Jews" clearly refers to specific Jews (including many of the Jewish leaders) who were opposed to Jesus' mission (see John 7:13). This is similar to how a modern person might use terms like *the Americans* or *the Republicans* to refer to national or party leadership. So, even though John says, "He came to his own home, and his own people received him not" (John 1:11), John is not saying that all Jews rejected Jesus.

In the next verse, John declares, "But to all who received him, who believed in his name, he gave power to become children of God." The New Testament does not teach that Judaism is something Christians should vilify, because Jesus affirmed that "salvation is from the Jews" (4:22). St. Paul declares that God has not abandoned the Jewish people (Rom. 11:1) and expresses his hope that, even though a part of Israel has rejected the Messiah in the future, "all Israel will be saved" (Rom. 11:26).[105]

. . . Jesus Fulfilled Messianic Prophecies

The reason we refer to Jesus of Nazareth as *Jesus Christ* is because *Christ* comes from a Greek title that means "Anointed One." (This is also why Jesus is sometimes called *the Christ* or simply, *Christ*). In ancient Judaism, the term was *mashiach*, or in English, *Messiah*. Israel's kings, priests, and prophets were anointed with oil (1 Kings 19:16 Lev. 4:3) and so they were considered messiahs and charged with leading God's people.[106]

But when most people talk about "the Messiah" they refer to the person, prophesied in the Old Testament, who would come and usher in an age of peace and restore the kingdom of David. The prophecies include, among many others, promises that he would be descended from David (Isa. 11:1), inaugurate a new covenant (Jer. 31:31), suffer for our sins (Isa. 53:5), conquer death (Isa. 25:8), and usher in an age of peace in which all people know the true God (Isa. 2:5, 11:9). Later rabbinic interpretations of the Old Testament have also held that the Messiah would bring about the reconstruction of the temple in Jerusalem, which was destroyed in A.D. 70.

The New Testament shows how Jesus fulfilled messianic prophecies related to his birth in Bethlehem (Micah 5:2, Matt. 2:4–6) and his entry into Jerusalem while riding a donkey (Zech. 9:9, John 12:14–15). When the high priest asked Jesus if he was the Messiah, Jesus answered, "I am; and you will see the Son of Man sitting at the right hand of Power, and coming with the clouds of heaven" (Mark 14:62).

Finally, when the risen Christ appeared to Cleopas and his companion on the road to Emmaus, he spoke to them of his own crucifixion (which they were lamenting) and asked, "Was it not necessary that the Christ should suffer these things and enter into his glory?" (Luke 24:26). Luke then tells us, "And beginning with Moses and all the prophets, he interpreted to them in all the scriptures the things concerning himself" (Luke 24:26–27).

Modern Jews usually reject Jesus as the Messiah because they say either he failed to fulfill genuine messianic prophecies or the Old Testament passages that Jesus did fulfill aren't actually messianic prophecies at all. The proper interpretation of Isaiah 53 is an example of the latter objection. It describes a "suffering servant" who would be wounded for our transgressions and by his wounds heal us (v. 5). He would be like "a lamb that is led to the slaughter" (v. 7) and assigned a grave with the wicked (v. 9). But ultimately this servant would "make many to be accounted righteous; and he shall bear their iniquities" (v. 11).

The earliest Fathers of the Church, such as Justin Martyr, saw these descriptions of a suffering servant fulfilled in Christ's passion and death.[107] But Jewish critics like Gerald Sigal claim that "the history of Israel, down through the ages, shows that the servant is none other than Israel personified."[108] But although Israel was often punished for its own sins or was the victim of other people's sins, neither the Bible nor Jewish history describes the nation of Israel atoning for other people's sins, as the suffering servant does in Isaiah 53.

In addition, the earliest Jewish sources after the time of Christ, like the rabbinic Talmud and Aramaic summaries of Scripture called *Targums*, all identified the text as referring not to a nation but to an individual, and in many cases that individual was the Messiah.[109] According to Michael Brown in his book *Answering Jewish Objections to Jesus*:

> How tempting it would have been for the Talmudic rabbis and their successors to interpret this passage with reference to Israel—rather than to the Messiah or any other individual—seeing that it played such an important role in Christian interpretation and polemics. Yet they did not interpret the passage with reference to the nation of Israel in any recorded traditional source for almost one thousand years, nor did they interpret it with reference to national Israel with unanimity thereafter.[110]

. . . Jesus Surpasses All Other Messiah Claimants

Observant Jews often claim that Jesus is not the Messiah because he did not rebuild the temple in Jerusalem. But although Christ did not rebuild that temple made of stone, he did "raise up" something even better: his own body, which would become the final and perfect sacrifice to which all the temple sacrifices were a precursor (c.f. Heb. 10:10).

N.T. Wright points out how "God's house in Jerusalem was meant to be a 'place of prayer for all the nations' (Isa. 56:7; Mark 11:17); but God would now achieve this though the new temple, which was Jesus himself and his people."[111] Christ's resurrection also fulfilled his promise to the Jewish authorities: "Destroy this temple, and in three days I will raise it up." John tells us Jesus was referring to "the temple of his body" (John 2:19–21), and Paul makes it clear that all believers make up "the body of Christ" (1 Cor. 12:27) and have become "temples of the Holy Spirit" (1 Cor. 6:19).

Pinchas Lapide is an orthodox Jew who believes that Jesus rose from the dead based on the historical and biblical evidence. He points out, "If the defeated and depressed group of disciples overnight could change into a victorious movement of faith, based only on autosuggestion or self-deception—without a fundamental faith experience—then this would be a much greater miracle than the Resurrection itself."[112]

Lapide does not believe that Jesus is the Messiah, though, because he doesn't think that Jesus has truly brought the kingdom of God into the world. This, however, makes a premature judgment based solely on Christ's first coming. Christians have long held that the Old Testament describes the Messiah coming twice—once as a suffering and rejected servant (Isa. 53) and again as a liberating king (Isa. 11). Just because Jesus has not fulfilled prophecies about world peace (Isa. 11) and the conquering of death (Isa. 25) doesn't mean he is not the Messiah because he can fulfill them at his Second Coming.

Even some Jews from before the time of Christ believed in two comings of the messiah, though it involved two different messiahs. For example, the original Hebrew text of Zechariah 6:11 refers to *crowns* (plural) being made for the king and priest involved in building the temple. And the first-century apocryphal Jewish work *The Testament of Simon* says:

> My children, obey Levi, and in Judah shall you be redeemed: and be not lifted up against these two tribes, for from them shall arise to you the salvation of God. For the Lord shall raise up from Levi as it were a priest, and from Judah as it were a king, God and man. So shall he save all the Gentiles and the race of Israel.[113]

We should also note that Isaiah 11:9 promises that through the Messiah, "the earth shall be full of the knowledge of the LORD as the waters cover the sea." In the first century there were probably about eight million Jews and less than 10,000 Christians out of a global population of approximately 300 million.[114] That means that less than three percent of the population had knowledge of the one true God and only .00003 percent possessed the fullness of God's self-revelation as the Father, Son, and Holy Spirit. Today, one-third of the world's population is Christian and more than half the population (including Jews and Muslims) professes belief in the God of Abraham.[115]

As we saw in our discussion of the evidence for the Resurrection, there have been many people throughout Jewish history who claimed to be the Messiah. In the time of Jesus this included Theudas and "the Egyptian," and more recently it has included people like Sabattai Sevi (1626-1676) and Lubavitcher Rebbe (1902-1994). However, none of these Messiah claimants have come anywhere as close as

Jesus Christ has to fulfilling the prophecy about causing the knowledge of God to be spread across the face of the earth. Even Lapide admits:

> The experience of the Resurrection as the foundation act of the Church which has carried the faith in the God of Israel into the whole Western world must belong to God's plan of salvation. . . . Since this Christianizing is based irrevocably on the resurrection of Jesus, the Easter faith has to be recognized as part of Divine Providence.[116]

Ironically, one good refutation of the counterfeit "misunderstood rabbi" Jesus can be found in the late Jacob Neusner's book *A Rabbi Talks with Jesus*. He points out how Jesus was not like other rabbis who grounded their authority in their interpretations of the ultimate authority for God's people: the Torah. Instead, Jesus made *himself* that ultimate authority through which the Torah was understood, which leads Neusner to conclude:

> Jesus was not just another reforming rabbi, out to make life "easier" for people. . . . It is disinguous to offer Jesus a standing, within Judaism, that Christianity rightly finds trivial and beside the point. If not Messiah, God incarnate, then to what grand issue of faith does my affirmation of a rabbi's or a prophet's teaching pertain?[117]

In his response to Neusner, Pope Benedict XVI noted, "The issue that is really at the heart of the debate is thus finally laid bare. Jesus understands himself as the Torah—as the Word of God in person."[118]

If Jesus is the Messiah, if he is God incarnate, then we should put our faith in him and realize how the law has been fulfilled with the Incarnation of the almighty lawgiver. Far from rejecting Judaism, the New Testament teaches that faith in Jesus as the Messiah, the one Scripture says would be called "Mighty God" (Isa. 9:6), fulfills the promises that were first given to the Jewish people (Rom. 3:2).

That's why Paul could say, "There is neither Jew nor Greek, there is neither slave nor free, there is neither male nor female; for you are all one in Christ Jesus. And if you are Christ's, then you are Abraham's offspring, heirs according to promise" (Gal. 3:28–29).

Prophet Named Isa

Before my first trip to Israel, I studied as much Hebrew as I could, but I ended up only using it at the Western Wall to tell people who mistook me for a local, "I'm sorry, I don't speak Hebrew." For everywhere else I went, it would have been more practical to speak Arabic. For the past three years, in fact, the most popular name in Israel for baby boys is Muhammad, which is the name of the prophet who founded the religion of Islam in the seventh century.[119]

Muhammad claimed to have recorded a revelation from God in what is now called the *Quran* (sometimes written *Koran;* it means "recitation") and is the sacred text of Islam. The fundamental claim of this revelation is that there is only God (*Allah*) and that Muhammad is his prophet or messenger. Islam teaches that it is the completion of the revelation God previously gave in the Bible, and accordingly the Quran describes stories involving people like Abraham and even Jesus (who in Arabic is called *Isa*).

Muslims are adamant that there is only one God and that God does not have a son. They say Jesus is not the Son of God but a prophet who, though he was born of a virgin, did not rise from the dead or proclaim himself to be divine. In fact, when our pilgrim group arrived at one holy site, we saw draped across from it a banner with Arabic verses from the Quran accompanied by this English translation:

> O People of the Scripture, do not commit excess in your religion or say about Allah except the truth. The Messiah, Jesus, the son of Mary, was but a messenger of Allah and his word which he directed to Mary and a soul [created at a command] from him. So believe in Allah and his messengers. And do not say, "Three"; desist—it is better for you (4:171).[120]

But how can that be true if . . .
. . . There's No Good Reason to Trust the Quran

The late Christian apologist Nabeel Qureshi said he converted from Islam because he asked himself, "What reason is there to stand by the koranic claims about Jesus when all the other records disagree? The Quran was written 600 years after Jesus and 600 miles away. The only reason to believe the Quran is an *a priori* faith in Islam."[121] In his analysis of all the non-biblical references to Jesus, Robert Van Voorst concludes of the Quran, "Scholarship has almost unanimously agreed that these references to Jesus are so late and tendentious as to contain virtually nothing of value for understanding the historical Jesus."[122]

In other words, because the Quran is so far removed from the historical events it purports to describe, the only reason to trust its testimony would be if it were the inspired word of God. But Muhammad never claimed to have performed any miracles that would vindicate his prophetic claims so there is no reason to believe the Quran is inspired. The Quran even admits that no sign or miracle had been given to confirm Muhammad's message. Sura (Quran verse) 13:7 says, "[T]hose who disbelieved say, 'Why has a sign not been sent down to him from his Lord?'" to which God tells Muhammad, "You are only a warner, and for every people is a guide."

The Quran does offer one proof for the validity of its own testimony. Sura 2:23 says that "if you are in doubt about what we have sent down upon Our Servant [Muhammad], then produce a sura the like thereof and call upon your witnesses other than Allah, if you should be truthful." In other words, "If you don't trust the Quran, try to write something better."

Muslim scholar Meraj Ahmad describes this "argument from literary eloquence" this way: "[N]o one has been able to imitate [the Quran's] unique literary form. [What] makes the Quran a miracle, is that it lies outside the productive capacity of the nature of the Arabic language and literature."[123]

Does it follow that just because something can't be imitated it must have a divine origin? The works of Shakespeare or Dostoevsky are unique and inimitable, but that doesn't mean God dictated them. Second, despite Muslim claims to the contrary, the Quran *is* similar to other medieval Arabic works and in some respects even deficient in comparison with them. According to the late Iranian author Ali Dashti:

> The Qo'ran [*sic*] contains sentences which are incomplete and not fully intelligible without the aid of commentaries . . . illogically and ungrammatically applied pronouns which sometimes have no referent; and predicates which in rhymed passages are often remote from the subjects. These and other such aberrations in the language have given scope to critics who deny the Qo'ran's eloquence.[124]

. . . The Quran Contradicts Scientific
and Historical Facts

Some Muslim apologists claim that the Quran contains scientific truths that wouldn't be discovered for centuries, and so could have only come from divine inspiration. But this requires generous and creative imposition of modern scientific knowledge on vague quranic descriptions of the natural world. For example, when it is said that the quranic verse about how God "creates you in the wombs of your mothers, creation after creation, within three darknesses" (39:6), refers to the linings of the abdomen, uterus, and amniotic sac.

Despite the arguments some apologists make for its scientific accuracy, there are several verses that appear to contradict modern science. One of these is the Quran's description of semen being created not from the testicles but "from between the backbone and the ribs" (86:7). Texts like these do not necessarily *disprove* the Quran because, like the Bible, it might be a divinely inspired text that speaks through ancient worldviews and does not claim to assert modern scientific truths. But they do cast doubt on the idea that the Quran contains miraculous scientific knowledge that could have only come from God and that this is proof of its trustworthiness.

One of the most glaring inaccuracies in the Quran, though, is not scientific but historical. Aside from mythicists who believe Jesus Christ never existed, Muslims are the only group who deny the well-accepted fact that Jesus died by crucifixion. The Quran says in Sura 4:157:

> And [for] their saying, "Indeed, we have killed the Messiah, Jesus, the son of Mary, the messenger of Allah." And they did not kill him, nor did they crucify him; but [another] was made to resemble him to them. And indeed,

those who differ over it are in doubt about it. They have no knowledge of it except the following of assumption. And they did not kill him, for certain.

This should make us seriously doubt the reliability of the Quran, because almost everyone, including non-Christians, agree that Jesus was crucified and died. Skeptical Bible scholar John Dominic Crossan denies that Jesus rose from the dead, but even he says "that he was crucified is as sure as anything historical can ever be."[125]

In response to this evidence, most Muslims believe that God only made it *appear* that Jesus was crucified by putting someone who looked like Jesus on the cross in his place. In the seventh century, Mohammed's cousin Ibn Abbas said this person was a Roman soldier named Tatianos or Natyanus.[126] But since, as we've seen, the Quran was written too late to be a reliable historical source about Jesus, "and since there is no evidence that it is divinely inspired," it follows that there are no reasons to believe its testimony when it contradicts the established historical record. This may be why some Muslim scholars claim Jesus was indeed crucified, but not "to death."[127]

Some modern Muslim apologists, like Shabir Ally and the late Ahmed Deedat, claim that God allowed Jesus to be crucified but that Jesus was "rescued" from death and so he wasn't crucified in *that* sense.[128] But it seems implausible that God would wait to "rescue" his beloved prophet until after he had been tortured, crucified, and then entombed. Also, most translators of the Quran recognize that the text makes a distinction between killing and crucifixion—and that it denies that *either* of these things happened to Jesus. The key passage in Sura 4:157 is thus rendered in most translations, "they did not kill him, nor did they crucify him."[129]

. . . The Quran Supports the Bible

Even if we grant a Muslim apologist that the Quran is without error and completely trustworthy, there is still a problem with the claim that we should deny Christian doctrines like the divinity of Christ. That's because the Quran tells us that the Gospels (in Arabic, the *injeel*) are a part of divine revelation and we should listen to *that* revelation too.

Sura 3:3 says, "He has sent down upon you, [O Muhammad], the Book in truth, confirming what was before it. And He revealed the Torah and the Gospel." The Quran says that Jews who do not follow the Hebrew Bible are like donkeys who carry heavy books but do not understand them (Sura 62:3). Christians are also exhorted to follow the New Testament, or as Sura 5:47 puts it, "[L]et the People of the Gospel judge by what Allah has revealed therein. And whoever does not judge by what Allah has revealed—then it is those who are the defiantly disobedient."

But this creates a contradiction because, as we saw in earlier chapters, the Bible teaches that Jesus is fully divine. In response to this problem, Muslim apologists claim the parts of the Bible that contradict the Quran are either misinterpreted by Christians or that they are textual corruptions added to the Bible later, and so not a part of Allah's original revelation. In order to bolster their argument, they often appeal to skeptical biblical scholars like Bart Ehrman.

We've already discussed the outstanding manuscript evidence showing that the New Testament could not have been corrupted (intentionally or accidentally) by anyone. I have also addressed Bart Ehrman's claim about the Bible's textual corruption at greater length in other works.[130] Here, let us focus on how Ehrman's own scholarship undermines the Muslim claim that the New Testament only teaches Muslim doctrines.

One Muslim apologetics website claims that in John 20:28 the apostle Thomas is not calling Jesus "God" even though he clearly says, "My Lord and my God!" They say Thomas is only saying that Jesus is "like God," because one ancient manuscript, called the *Codex Bezae*, omits the Greek direct article *ho* before the Greek word for God (*theos*). They claim:

> The predecessor of the *Codex Bezae* and other Church manuscripts do not contain the article "*Ho*" ("THE") in their text (*The Orthodox Corruption of Scripture*, Bart D. Ehrman, p. 266). What this means is that this verse in its original form, if it is to be understood to be addressing Jesus (peace be upon him) himself, only addresses him as "divine" and not as the "Almighty God." Thus, it is similar in meaning to the meaning conveyed when prophet Moses is described as being a "god" in Exodus 7:1.[131]

So, according to this apologist, the absence of the definite article *ho* before the Greek word for God proves that Thomas addressed Jesus as a mighty prophet of God but not the mighty, true God himself. But this misuses Ehrman's scholarship to support the view that the *Codex Bezae* records what John originally wrote.

Every other ancient manuscript records Thomas using the definite article and saying to Jesus, "The Lord of me and the God of me" [*ho kyrios mou kai ho theos mou*]. New Testament professor Brian Wright points out that the *Codex Bezae* "is an eccentric manuscript and regularly drops the article," so it probably doesn't reflect the original reading of John 20:28. Ehrman conjectures that the scribe who copied the *Codex Bezae* intentionally left out the article *ho* and kept *theos* in order to thwart heretics who claimed that Jesus and the Father were the same person (a heresy that still persists and we will address in chapter 12).

So this is just evidence that an overzealous scribe in the fifth century incorrectly copied previous manuscripts, not that those manuscripts or the original text of John 20:28 does not affirm the divinity of Christ. Moreover, as Wright points out, even if the original text lacked the definite article before *theos*, he shows that Granville Sharp's Rule (which we learned about in chapter 3) would apply, thus making it undeniable that Jesus is identified as *theos,* or the one God, in this verse.[132] In fact, the Muslim apologist's reliance on Bart Ehrman will come back to haunt him, because elsewhere Ehrman states, "[T]he Gospel of John—in which Jesus does make such divine claims—does indeed portray him as God."[133]

If the Quran says we can trust the revelation God gave to St. John, and John describes Jesus as being God incarnate, then we should conclude that Jesus is not just a prophet that God sent to be a forerunner to Muhammad. He is instead the God who sent all the prophets and now comes to manifest himself to us, or as the letter to the Hebrews tells us:

> In many and various ways God spoke of old to our fathers by the prophets; but in these last days he has spoken to us by a Son, whom he appointed the heir of all things, through whom also he created the world. He reflects the glory of God and bears the very stamp of his nature, upholding the universe by his word of power (1:1–3).

9

New Age Guru

Deepak Chopra is an alternative medicine doctor and self-help advocate whose advice sounds profound but, upon closer examination, turns out to be verbose gibberish. For example, consider these two quotes:

> "Attention and intention are the mechanics of manifestation."

> "Your consciousness quiets an expression of knowledge."

The former is a real Chopra quote; the latter is just a random combination of words strung together by an online "Deepak Chopra quote generator."[134] It's hard to tell them apart because Chopra's "wisdom" consists of vague assertions about the mind creating reality combined with scientific jargon. In one article he claims, "Quantum theory implies that consciousness must exist, and that the content of the mind is the ultimate reality. If we do not look at it, the moon is gone."[135]

Lest you think Chopra is being merely poetic, he really believes that the most fundamental element of reality is consciousness and that we *create* the world around us (including the moon). He says that once we attain a high level of consciousness we can manipulate reality and accomplish incredible feats, like healing ourselves of cancer.[136] When it comes to Jesus, Chopra promotes a common Eastern view of him as a "guru," or someone who had achieved a level of introspective knowledge that leads to human fulfillment.

In his book *The Third Christ*, Chopra says, "Jesus did not physically descend from God's dwelling place above the clouds, nor did he return to sit at the right hand of a literal throne. What made Jesus the Son of God was the fact that he has achieved God-consciousness."[137] So Jesus is God in the sense that we are *all* "God," or that we all have the spark of "God-consciousness" within us, waiting to be actualized. That's why Chopra tells us, "Jesus intended to save the world" not by dying for our sins but, "by showing others the path to God-consciousness."[138]

But how can that be true if . . .
. . . "Guru Jesus" Is Unhistorical

In his 2008 book *Jesus: A Story of Enlightenment,* Chopra weaves a fanciful tale to explain how Jesus became so "enlightened." He takes advantage of the thirty years of Christ's life between his birth and the start of his public ministry that are not described in Scripture (save for when Jesus' parents found him in the Temple at the age of twelve) to claim that during his teens and twenties Jesus went on a journey to India, where he learned the secret of enlightenment from other wise men before returning to Galilee.

Chopra's tale is just another in a long line of speculative stories about Christ's "hidden years." They go all the way back to medieval writers, who imagined a young Jesus visiting England with his traveling-tin-merchant father Joseph of Arimathea (an idea later popularized in William Blake's 1808 poem "And did those feet in ancient time"). The claim about Jesus going to India comes from Nicolas Notovitch's 1894 work *The Life of Saint Issa*, in which he claims to have seen an ancient document in a Himalayan monastery that describes how Jesus studied Buddhism in the region. But when other journalists went and visited this monastery, they learned Notovitch had never even been there. But it was a lucrative hoax for him.[139]

In his book, *Jesus Outside the New Testament*, Robert Van Voorst says that when it comes to Jesus' alleged travels to India and Tibet, they are as historically worthless as the Quran's testimony about Jesus we discussed in the previous chapter.[140] Chopra readily admits that there's no evidence for his theory in the Bible. After claiming that an unknown German scholar made these claims in the 1940s (whom Chopra may have mistaken for Notovitch) he concludes, "I went into incubation, meditation, and I allowed this story to unfold. It fits into the category of 'religious fiction.'"[141]

Chopra also appeals to the apocryphal Gospels, which do have Gnostic themes that are similar to New Age thought, as witnesses to the "mystical Jesus." For example, in the Gospel of Thomas, Jesus is made so say, "I am the light that is over all things. I am all: from me all came forth, and to me all attained. Split a piece of wood; I am there. Lift up the stone, and you will find me there" (77).

Some scholars claim that the Gospel of Thomas is a first-century work and so it is the most reliable of the bunch. But other scholars, including critical ones like Bart Ehrman, believe that the Gospel's allusions to other books of the New Testament, its reliance on later Syriac renderings of those texts, and its absence of apocalyptic themes place its composition in the middle of the second century. This alone would make it far less reliable than the first-century canonical Gospels.[142] And that leaves the Guru Jesus theory without any historical basis whatsoever.

. . . Jesus Preached Salvation, Not Enlightenment

Along with the total absence of evidence to corroborate Jesus' fabled trip to India, there is no evidence from the Bible that Jesus preached New Age principles of "enlightenment."

It's true that some of Jesus' ethical teachings are similar to those of Buddha, but this doesn't mean Jesus learned these teachings from the followers of Buddha. In *Jesus and Buddha: The Parallel Sayings*, New Testament scholar Marcus Borg calls explanations like that "unlikely and unnecessary. The similarities [between Jesus' and Buddha's teachings] are not of the kind that suggest cultural borrowing. They are not at the level of specific images and language."[143]

A more plausible explanation is that the fundamental elements of morality in the natural law can be known by anyone through the light of human reason. That explains why a variant of the Golden Rule in Luke 6:31 ("Do to others as you would have them do to you") can be found in many other cultures including Buddhism ("Consider others as yourself") and the Old Testament, ("You shall love him as yourself").[144]

But when it comes to theology, Buddha and Jesus are as different as night and day. For example, Eastern religions preach the need to adopt certain behaviors or attitudes in order to be "saved" from the afflictions we face in this life. In Buddhism this is called "Noble Eight-fold Path" which consists of practicing "right" kinds of view, intention, speech, conduct, likelihood, effort, mindfulness, and *Samadhi*, which is a kind of meditative consciousness.

This "path" does not include faith in the traditional Western view of God, and the Buddha himself rejected the existence of any such being.[145] Buddha did not verify the truth of his teachings with miraculous works; in fact he denounced such methods.[146] He also did not consider himself a "personal savior" who could deliver people from their suffering. On the contrary, Buddha exhorted others to "be islands (or lamps) unto yourselves, refuges unto yourselves, seeking no external refuge."[147]

Now compare this to Jesus, who said, "I am the light of the world. Whoever follows me will not walk in darkness, but will have the light of life" (John 8:12). Jesus also reassured his disciples that they should believe him *because* of his miraculous deeds. He said, "The Father who dwells in me does his works. Believe me that I am in the Father and the Father in me; or else believe me for the sake of the works themselves" (John 14:10–11). What made Jesus unique were not his teachings about the way we should live or the truths we should believe. Rather, it was his teaching about *himself* being "the way" and "the truth" and how it is only through him we can gain access to the Father and have eternal life (John 14:6).

So what does Chopra do with evidence from the Bible that shows Jesus was not a "God-conscious" guru but the Son of God sent to save us from sin? He simply dismisses as unreliable anything that contradicts his thesis. He even derides the attempt to know the real Jesus as a "fundamentalist effort."[148] But then a few paragraphs later Chopra proceeds to tell us "the real Jesus is as available today as he ever was," because *that* Jesus lives in our own consciousness.[149]

We'll examine Chopra's efforts to use the Bible to support this view of Christ, but keep in mind that even radical skeptics have criticized Chopra's manhandling of Scripture.

Robert Price (who denies that Jesus existed) accuses Chopra of not bothering to check his sources and notes how Chopra fabricates Bible verses like, "Inspiration is an act of grace." As a result, Price exhorts his readers, "when trying to decide whether to take the diagnosis of Dr. Chopra, I would seek a second opinion!"[150]

. . . "Guru Exegesis" Misinterprets Scripture

Recall Chopra's claim, "What made Jesus the Son of God was the fact that he has achieved God-consciousness." He defends this assertion by saying, "Jesus said as much, over and over, when he declared that 'the Father and I are one' (John 10:30). [Jesus] knew no separation between his thoughts and God's thoughts, his feelings and God's feelings, his actions and the actions God wanted performed."[151]

But Jesus was not saying he had simply reached a higher spiritual level through meditation or other human endeavors. We know because in the very next verses John tells us:

> The Jews took up stones again to stone him. Jesus answered them, "I have shown you many good works from the Father; for which of these do you stone me?" The Jews answered him, "We stone you for no good work but for blasphemy; because you, being a man, make yourself God."

In an interview about his book, Chopra noted how the crowd wanted to stone Jesus for saying this, but imagines that Jesus' response to them actually vindicates his position. Chopra says, "But [Jesus] quotes a psalm that says 'You are Gods, sons of the most high,' (John 10:34) which he tells them was addressed to 'those to whom the word of God came.' He clearly sees himself as equivalent to that group."[152]

In other words, Jesus was saying that he is God, but that's not blasphemy because we are all "God" in the sense that we all have God-consciousness within us.

Did Jesus teach that we are all literal "gods in training" as Mormons, who also cite this verse, believe? Not any more than he taught we are all gods because we have "God-consciousness" within us.

The Jews reveal that they want to stone Jesus, making the accusation: "You, being a man, make yourself God" (John 10:33). Jesus then points out that in Scripture human beings are called gods: "God has taken his place in the divine council; in the midst of the gods he holds judgment" (Psalm 82:1). The Hebrew word for God, or *elohim*, is sometimes used to refer to human judges (Exod. 22:9). Jesus quotes Psalm 82 because it criticizes human judges, like the Pharisees, who were wicked and fell short of the moral standard set by God. Psalm 82:7 even says those "elohim" will "die like men," so we know that these beings were not actual gods.

According to the *Catholic Commentary on Holy Scripture*, in this passage Jesus is using a rabbinic form of argument called *qal wahōmer*, which means "from the less to the greater." It says:

> Jesus does not deny the charge [of calling himself God], nor mitigate what he has said, but leads them to reason upward from a Scripture text. . . . "I said: 'You are gods . . . '" The appellation is God's own and registered in an inviolable Scripture. Therefore, a fortiori, it is not blasphemy to apply it to one of higher dignity. That one is Jesus whom the Father has consecrated and sent into the world, as his anointed, holy Envoy.[153]

Jesus does not explicitly declare his divinity in the presence of his critics, but he does artfully refute their argument while leaving the door open for those who do believe in him to see the complete meaning of his response. That's why in the next verse Jesus tells his listeners that even if his words do not persuade them his works should: "Believe the works, that you may know and understand that the Father is in me and I am in the Father" (John 10:37).

Jesus' claims might seem blasphemous, but they are vindicated by the fact that, unlike other famous rabbis who performed miracles by asking God to do things like heal someone or send rain, Jesus simply performed those mighty works by his own authority, which came from his unique identity as the only begotten Son of God.

Chopra also tries to bolster this New Age interpretation with Jesus' words in Luke 17:21, which the KJV renders, "The kingdom of God is within you." Modern translations usually render this passage, "The kingdom of God is *in the midst* of you" [Greek: *he basileia tou theou entos hymon estin*]. But even if the Greek word translated "in the midst" (*entos*) does mean "within" or "inside," we shouldn't conclude that the kingdom of God exists *in the consciousness* of individual believers.

The previous verse says that the Pharisees asked Jesus when the kingdom of God was coming. Jesus answered them, "The kingdom of God is not coming with signs to be observed. Nor will they say, 'Lo, here it is!' or 'There!'" In other words, God's kingdom would not be a visible, earthly kingdom like David's. As he would later tell Pontius Pilate, his kingdom would "not be of this world" (John 19:38) but would be an invisible, spiritual kingdom. The kingdom is not *generated* within us through Eastern practices like meditation but is instead *received* within us from a God who exists apart from our own consciousness.

Ephrem the Syrian said Luke 17:21 refers to "the heavenly joy of the Spirit being active in the soul that is worthy of it" and Origen said it referred to the Logos, God's very Word, dwelling in our souls.[154] This corresponds to when Jesus promised, "If a man loves me, he will keep my word, and my Father will love him, and we will come to him and make our home with him" (John 14:23) and St. Paul's prayer that, "Christ may dwell in your hearts through faith" (Eph. 3:17).

"Guru exegesis" perverts the meaning of the gospel because it takes the mystery of God humbly coming down to humanity to save us and replaces it with us going "up" to him through our own clever consciousness-raising. This is evident in Chopra's reassurance, "You don't need to have faith in the Messiah or his mission. Instead, you have faith in the vision of higher consciousness" and his baffling claim that "'I' and 'God' become one and the same."[155]

But when we think about the times we've failed others and ourselves, all the times we apologize and say, "This isn't who I am," we testify to the reality that we only possess a tarnished image of God within us. We are *not* God, and we can't save ourselves through our own efforts. Instead, we must turn to the perfect standard of goodness himself and remember that he said, "I am the vine, you are the branches. He who abides in me, and I in him, he it is that bears much fruit, for apart from me you can do nothing" (John 15:5).

COUNTERFEITS
from
Quasi-Christians

10

Jehovah's Greatest Creation

The doorbell rings, and you peer through the peephole. Standing on your doorstep is a man in a suit and a woman in a tasteful dress. They don't look like your average salespeople, so you open the door.

It turns out they are here today to see if you "hope for a better world" or if you "wonder if the Bible is still relevant." They offer you some free magazines and let you know they're willing to study the Bible with you at your convenience. You soon learn that the guests on your doorstep are Jehovah's Witnesses, part of a religious group founded in the 1870s that has nearly eight million members worldwide.[156] And they have their own counterfeit version of Jesus.

The central belief of Jehovah's Witnesses is that there is one God and his name is *Jehovah*. According to them, Jehovah created a "Son" and it was through this Son that he created the rest of the world. This Son, whom we now call Jesus, has the same "spirit nature" as his Father, which makes him "a god" or "a mighty god." However, the Son is still a creation of the Father, and so he is not the "true God" and should not be worshipped. As their *Awake!* magazine says, "[T]rue Christians do well to direct their worship only to Jehovah God, the Almighty."[157]

Since the Witnesses believe that Jesus is the highest or most glorious of God's creatures, and they consider archangels to be the highest of the angels, it follows for them that Jesus must be an archangel. And since Michael is called "*the* archangel," that means there is only one archangel and so Michael and Jesus must be the same.[158] They further claim:

> The only other verse in which an archangel is mentioned is at 1 Thessalonians 4:16, where Paul describes the resurrected Jesus, saying: 'The Lord [Jesus] himself will descend from heaven with a commanding call, with an archangel's voice and with God's trumpet.' So Jesus Christ himself is here identified as the archangel, or chief angel.[159]

But how can that be true if . . .
. . . The Bible Says That Jesus Is Not an Angel

Calling Michael *the* archangel in Jude 1:9 doesn't prove that Michael is the only archangel any more than calling Sonic *the* Hedgehog proves he is the only hedgehog. Neither does describing Jesus as descending "with an archangel's voice" require us to conclude that he is an archangel. (The same verse also says that Jesus will descend with God's trumpet, but that doesn't mean Jesus is a trumpet.) It only means that Jesus' voice will have the quality of an archangel's voice, or that he will be accompanied by angels who will shout for him.

Besides, the Bible explicitly teaches that Jesus is superior to all the angels, including the archangels. Hebrews 1:4–6 says Jesus has:

become as much *superior to angels* as the name he has obtained is more excellent than theirs. For to what angel did God ever say, "Thou art my Son, today I have begotten thee"? Or again, "I will be to him a father, and he shall be to me a son"? And again, when he brings the firstborn into the world, he says, *"Let all God's angels worship him."*

Angels don't worship other angels; they worship only God. Since Jehovah's Witnesses believe that Jesus is Michael the archangel, their New World Translation of the Bible (NWT) avoids the situation of angels worshipping another angel by rendering this passage, "Let all of God's angels do obeisance to him."

Obeisance means to bow down in respect for another person. In Exodus 18:7, Moses made obeisance to his father-in-law, Jethro; and in 1 Kings 1:16, Bathsheba bowed before King David. These instances of obeisance merely describe paying solemn respect to someone. They do not describe the kind of worship one would give to God.

The Greek word in Hebrews 1:6 that Jehovah's Witnesses translate "obeisance" is *proskuneo*. This word can indeed refer to simple bowing or showing a sign of respect to someone in authority. But, it can also refer to the kind of worship given to God alone. Interestingly, elsewhere the NWT renders *proskuneo* as "worship" when the verb has God the Father as its direct object (e.g., John 4:20–23). It even translates it as "worship" when it is used to describe the worship of a false god, such as the Beast in Revelation 13. But when *proskuneo* is used of Jesus, the NWT always translates it as "obeisance" and never as "worship."

This may be appropriate in verses that describe people paying respect to Jesus, such as when the mother of James and John kneel before Jesus before requesting that he give her sons special authority (Matt. 20:20). But there are other verses where context makes it clear that *worship* is the most appropriate word to use. This includes Luke 24:52 and Matthew 28:9, both of which refer to the apostles worshipping Jesus after his resurrection.

After Jesus calmed the storm on the Sea of Galilee, Matthew 14:33 tells us, "Those in the boat worshipped him, saying, 'Truly you are the Son of God.'" In the Old Testament, only God possessed power over the weather and the sea. Biblical scholar Moran Hooker points out that even though the disciples ask, "Who then is this, that even wind and sea obey him?" (Mark 4:41), to the reader of the Gospel "the answer to their question is obvious. It is God who made the sea, and God alone who controls it (Ps. 89:8). The authority with which Jesus acts is that of God himself."[160]

. . . The Apostle John Says That Jesus Is God

Jehovah's Witnesses often says Jesus is "*a* god," but not "the true God." But that raises the question: "If Jesus is not the true God, is he a false god?" The New Testament never says Jesus is "a god" or merely "a mighty god." In fact, John describes Jesus as the Word made flesh (John 1:14) and declares in the first verse of his Gospel, "In the beginning was the Word, and the Word was with God, and the Word was God" (John 1:1). Because this verse identifies Jesus as God, however, the NWT translates it, "In the beginning was the Word, and the Word was with God, and the Word was *a* God."

Jehovah's Witnesses are taught early in their Bible studies to say something like this in response to John 1:1: "The correct translation is 'The Word was a god' not 'The Word was God.' That's because the Greek word for *God* in this passage, *theos*, does not have the Greek article [the word *the*] in front of it in the original text."

It's true that the original Greek text of John 1:1 does not have the Greek word for *the* before "God." However, that doesn't mean that the indefinite article *a* should be put there instead. Greek doesn't have indefinite articles, so translators insert them based on the context of the passage. The Witnesses simply assume that in this context the Word is not God.

Yet they don't consistently follow their own rules of translation. Just a few verses later, the evangelist says of John the Baptist, "There came a man who was sent as a representative of God [*theos*]; his name was John" (1:6). Just like in John 1:1, *theos* lacks the definite article, but here it is not translated as "a God." In their defense of the divinity of Christ, Robert Bowman and J. Ed Komosewski note:

> If John had meant to signal that *ho theos* meant "God" and *theos* meant "a god," his wording in the rest of the prologue (John 1:1–18) is very strange. After verse 2, which summarizes the first two clauses of verse 1, *theos* appears five times in the prologue, each time without the article, and in the first four occurrences everyone agrees it means "God" (vv. 6, 12, 13, 18a, 18b).[161]

We've seen how John also records Jesus using the sacred divine name ("I am"), which confirms that Jesus is the eternal Word that has become man (John 8:58). This verse is so contradictory to Jehovah's Witness theology that their Bible has Jesus say in John 8:58, "Before Abraham came into existence, I have been." According to them, Jesus was merely claiming *preexistence*, or being a very old part of Jehovah's creation. He was not claiming to be Jehovah himself, since he did not exactly utter the sacred divine name.

Is there a good reason to think that John 8:58 should be translated, "Before Abraham was, I have been" instead of "Before Abraham was, I am?"

In Greek, the verse reads, *prin Abraam genesthai ego eimi.* The part we are concerned with is the last part: *ego eimi.* *Ego* means "I," and *eimi* is the Greek word for the verb "to be." So where John 10:9 reads in Greek, *ego eimi he thyra*, we translate it as Jesus saying, "I am the door," not "I have been the door." *Ego eimi* is a simple phrase to translate in Greek, and it makes sense to translate in John 8:58 as "I am," not "I have been." In fact, the Greek translation of the Old Testament (called the *Septuagint*) describes God revealing his name to Moses in Exodus 3:14 as *ego eimi*, or, "I AM."

But what about when Jesus says, "The Father is greater than I" (John 14:28)? If Jesus is God, shouldn't he be *equal* to the Father?

Well, just because someone is described as being greater than another person does not mean that person is greater in *being,* as it is in the claim that humans are greater than plants. In Scripture this isn't the case. Among the apostles, for example, St. James the *Greater* (the son of Zebedee) and St. James the *Lesser* (possibly the Son of Alphaeus) possess titles that refer to the former being taller or older than the latter. It can also refer to one person having more authority or a higher position than another person.

When Jesus says the Father is "greater," he means that the Father holds a higher *position* than he does. Christ was in a "lesser" position than the Father during his earthly ministry because he set aside his divine glory in order to become man (Phil. 2:7). That's why Scripture says that during his earthly life, Jesus was for "a little while lower than the angels" (Heb. 2:7). But, after his resurrection, Jesus fully manifested his divine glory. As a result of this exaltation, God bestowed on him, "the name which is above every name, that at the name of Jesus every knee should bow, in heaven and on earth and under the earth, and every tongue confess that Jesus Christ is Lord, to the glory of God the Father" (Phil. 2:9–11).

Interestingly, whenever the word *Lord* (or *kurios*) is found in the New Testament, the NWT renders it "Jehovah"—*except* in verses like Philippians 2:11, where the title is applied to Jesus. For example, a *Watchtower* magazine article quotes Romans 10:13 as, "Everyone who calls on the name of Jehovah will be saved."[162] But Romans 10:13 doesn't contain the word *Jehovah*. It says, "Everyone who calls on the name of the LORD [*kuriou*] will be saved."

If the NWT were consistent, it would render Romans 10:9 as, "If you confess with your lips that Jesus is *Jehovah* and believe in your heart that God raised him from the dead, you will be saved." But this consistency would come at the expense of a theology that denies that Jesus is the true God named Jehovah (whom ancient Jews knew by the name *Yahweh* and not Jehovah).[163]

. . . Jesus Accepts Divine Worship

The fact that Jesus returns to his original status alongside the Father in order to sit at his "right hand" (Acts 7:55) means he has an equal position with the Father, which is indeed cause for rejoicing. The disciples should not mourn Jesus leaving, because Jesus is going to reign as their "Lord and God." In fact, after his resurrection, Jesus allows Thomas to call him, "My Lord and my God!" (John 20:28).

This is astonishing, because in the New Testament, whenever an apostle is mistaken for God he corrects those who are worshipping him (Acts 14:14–15). In Revelation 19:10, the apostle John falls at the feet of an angel to worship him, but the angel tells him, "You must not do that!" When Herod Agrippa (the grandson of Herod the Great who tried to kill Jesus when he was an infant) gives an address to the people of Tyre and Sidon they shout in response, "The voice of a god, and not of man!" Luke then tells us, "Immediately an angel of the Lord smote him, because he did not give God the glory; and he was eaten by worms and died" (Acts 12:23).

Yet Jesus did *not* correct Thomas or tell him to "give God the glory." No angel smote him. This should lead us to the conclusion that there was nothing to correct. Thomas's statement of faith speaks the truth. If that is the case, then we should imitate Thomas and not be afraid to address Jesus as our "Lord and God" as well.

Some Jehovah's Witnesses say that Thomas was so overcome with joy that he didn't know what he was saying. But in other Scripture passages we are told explicitly when the apostles say something they don't mean. After Jesus' transfiguration, for instance, Peter says impulsively that he will build tents for Jesus, Moses, and Elijah. In response to this exclamation, Luke describes Peter as "not knowing what he said" (Luke 9:33), while Mark says that Peter "did not know what to say, for they were exceedingly afraid" (Mark 9:6).

Jehovah's Witnesses also can't say that Thomas was merely making an exclamation, like how some people say, "Oh my God!" when they are surprised. Even in the NWT, John 20:28 says, "In answer Thomas said to him: 'My Lord and my God!'" So, Thomas didn't merely say, "My Lord and My God!" He said it *to* Jesus because Jesus is his (and our) Lord and God.

But what about just a few verses earlier, in John 20:17, when Jesus told Mary Magdelene, "I am ascending to my Father and your Father, to my God and your God"? How can Jesus be God if he calls another person God?

The answer is found in the doctrines of the Trinity and the Incarnation. One person can refer to another person as "God" if God is not a single person but a single, infinite act of being. Moreover, if one of these divine persons, such as the Son, became man and possessed a fully human nature, then, as a man, he would give worship to the Father and recognize the Father is God. As a result, there is nothing contradictory in Jesus being the "God-man" who prays to the Father and recognizes that the Father is "his God."

But notice that even in his exchange with Mary Magdalene, Jesus makes a distinction between "my Father" and "your Father" and "my God" and "your God" instead of just saying "our God" or "our Father." This implies that God is a Father to Mary Magdalene and the apostles in a different sense than he is a Father to Jesus. Specifically, they (and us) have God as an *adoptive* father (Romans 8:15), whereas Jesus is the only *begotten* Son of God (John 1:18).

We are *like* God because God gives us his grace as adopted children; but Jesus *is* God because he shares the same divine nature as the Father. This is important because if Jesus were merely an exalted man or angel, his death could not pay the infinite debt our sins incur against an infinitely holy God. Fortunately, Jesus is not "Jehovah's greatest creation"—he *is Jehovah*, the God of the Old Testament who became man so that there could be, "one mediator between God and men, the man Christ Jesus, who gave himself as a ransom for all" (1 Tim. 2:5–6).

Our Eldest Brother

Once a young woman sitting next to me on an airplane noticed I was reading a book about Mormonism. She said she had recently joined the Mormon Church (the official name for Mormons is "members of the Church of Jesus Christ of Latter-day Saints," which some people abbreviate to "LDS")[164] and so we struck up a conversation. She said she didn't like it when people held ignorant views toward Mormons and I agreed that bigoted attitudes are unacceptable.

"I mean, we all believe in Jesus, so isn't that what matters?" she asked.

I gently explained to her that Christians and Mormons don't mean the same thing when they refer to the person of Jesus. Gordon Hinkley, the former president of the Mormon Church, even said, "As a church we have critics, many of them. They say we do not believe in the traditional Christ of Christianity. There is some substance to what they say."[165]

Christians believe there is one God who exists as three divine, eternal persons: the Father, Son, and Holy Spirit, and that only God is eternal (see Psalm 90:2). Mormons, on the other hand, believe there are an infinite number of "intelligences" that have existed for all eternity. God, whom Mormons call "Heavenly Father," transforms these intelligences into human beings and the faithful Mormons among them will become gods in the next life, going on to create more human beings who will continue this cycle of "exaltation."[166]

Mormons believe that Jesus Christ was once an "intelligence" like us who existed from eternity past. He was not always divine, and he was not always the Son of God. Instead, God chose him to become the "firstborn" among the intelligences by giving him the first spirit body.[167] In 1909, the Mormon Church's leadership released a statement that read, "The Father of Jesus is our Father also. . . . Jesus, however, is the firstborn among all the sons of God—the first begotten in the spirit, and the only begotten in the flesh. He is our elder brother, and we, like him, are in the image of God."[168]

Instead of being completely different in *kind* from human beings, this counterfeit Christ is only different from us in *degree* (hence the term "eldest brother"). He is just a more exalted spirit-child of God the Father, which reduces him from being the eternal creator of the universe to being merely one highly praised part of it.

But how can that be true if . . .
. . . There Is Only One God

Mormonism can best be described as a kind of *henotheism*, or belief in the existence of many gods (in this case, infinitely many), only one of whom deserves our worship. Mormons strive to become "exalted" and develop into a god just like Heavenly Father, who was once a man like us. Joseph Smith even said at a funeral for Mormon elder King Follett, "You have got to learn how to be gods yourselves, and to be kings and priests to God, the same as all gods have done before you."[169]

Christians, on the other hand, are *monotheists* who believe there is one God, though he exists as a Trinity of three persons, each of whom equally possesses the divine nature.[170] And although Mormons will tell you that they, too, believe in "one God," what they mean is that they believe in one *collection* of gods. For Mormons, the Father, Son, and Holy Spirit (or "the Holy Ghost") are three gods who cooperate so perfectly they might as well be one God. But this is like saying that a perfectly cooperating baseball team has but one player.

If God or Heavenly Father used to be a man who was later exalted into godhood, then the entire universe would be without an explanation, because we could always ask the atheist's favorite question: "Who created God?" Positing an infinite cycle of men becoming gods does not explain the existence of the universe any more than an infinitely long chain could explain why a chandelier is hanging in a room.[171] It has to be attached to the ceiling, and likewise, the only explanation for why the universe exists at all is because the God of Christianity, who just is perfect existence itself, created it.

Scripture also clearly teaches there is only one God, and we are to worship him alone. There's no doubt that the early Israelites were also henotheists, because they were often tempted to worship other gods that they presumed really existed. But through gradual, divine revelation God's people came to understand that Yahweh was not only superior to all other gods—he was *real* and they were not. In Isaiah 45:5, God says, "I am the Lord, and there is no other, besides me there is no God."

In Isaiah 43:10 God declares, "Before me no god was formed, nor shall there be any after me." This can't refer to false gods or idols, because many of those are still "formed" to this day. Instead, the Bible teaches that no other god besides the one true God has ever existed, and no other god

ever will exist. Even scholars who reject evidence for practices of monotheism early in the Old Testament agree that
the prophet Isaiah is a witness to God's people having finally
rejected the existence of all other deities except for their
own God Yahweh.[172]

The New Testament also firmly teaches not just that Jesus
is God, but that there is only one God. Jesus described God
as "the only God" (John 5:44) and "the only true God"
(John 17:3). St. Paul describes God as "the only wise God"
(Rom. 16:27) and the only being who possesses immortality
(1 Tim. 6:16). St. Ignatius wrote in the early second century that the early Christians were persecuted because they
"convince the unbelieving that there is one God, who has
manifested himself by Jesus Christ his Son."[173]

If there is only one God, and the Father, the Son, and the
Holy Spirit are fully divine and distinct from one another
(which we will discuss in the next chapter), then the doctrine of the Trinity logically follows. Jesus could not have
been an "intelligence" that another god elevated to divinity,
but must instead be an inseparable part of the one, Triune
God who alone has eternal, necessary existence.

. . . The Bible Teaches That Jesus Created All Things

Mormons believe that the world is eternal—that it never had
a beginning—and God is just a being who exists within it.
The God of this world created it in the same way a baker
"creates" a cake—by combining pre-existing ingredients.
Eric Shuster, a Mormon convert from Catholicism, writes,
"Latter-day Saint doctrine holds that the universe was *formed*
and *organized*, not created *ex nihilo*, 'out of nothing' as Catholic doctrine holds. This is not an insignificant difference."[174]

Christians, on the other hand, have always believed that God created all things out of nothing at some point in the distant past. Hebrews 11:3 says that "the world was created by the word of God, so that what is seen was made out of things which do not appear" (in some other translations, "was not made out of visible things."). *The Shepherd of Hermas*, an early Christian writing from around the year A.D. 80, says, "First of all, believe that there is one God who created and finished all things, and made all things out of nothing. He alone is able to contain the whole, but himself cannot be contained."[175]

According to Mormonism, in the beginning Heavenly Father sent the pre-incarnate Jesus (whose name at that time was Jehovah) and the archangel Michael to form our world from pre-existing matter. But this contradicts Isaiah 44:24, where God says, "I am the LORD, who made all things, who stretched out the heavens alone, who spread out the earth—Who was with me?" Colossians 1:16–17 also tells us that it was through Jesus that *all things* were created, Jesus is before *all things*, and in Jesus *all things* hold together.[176]

If God was alone when he created all things, then he did not receive help from separate spiritual beings like Jesus or Michael the Archangel. And if he truly created *all* things, then he did not form anything from uncreated matter. Finally, if the New Testament tells us that Jesus created all things, and the Old Testament says that God alone created all things, this must mean that Jesus is the God of the Old Testament who would gradually come to be revealed as three distinct persons who exist as the one God that created the world.

Reducing Jesus from being our Creator to only our "eldest brother" leads to an interesting consequence: Jesus becomes not only *our* brother but the brother of Heavenly Father's other spirit children—which includes the fallen angel Lucifer.

Mormons say this doesn't mean that Jesus and Satan deserve the same respect, are similar in status, or that Mormons worship Satan. Nonetheless, Jesus and the devil are both God's spirit children—along with us.

Some Mormons cite the Bible's description of Jesus as "the firstborn among many brethren" (Rom. 8:29) and the "firstborn of creation" (Col. 1:15) as evidence that he was created to be our "eldest brother" and is not himself the eternal creator of all things.[177] But Romans 8:29 refers to how Jesus was the first human to take part in the glory of the *resurrection*—not that Jesus was created. That verse says God planned for others to be "conformed" to Christ's image, becoming his brethren by sharing in the future glory that he first received.

Regarding Colossians 1:15, the term *firstborn* doesn't always mean "the oldest child within a family." The Greek word for "firstborn," *prototokos*, can refer to a special position that is worthy of honor and privilege. For example, in Psalm 89:27 God says of David, "I will make him the firstborn, the highest of the kings of the earth." Obviously, David was not the first king ever to reign on earth. And we know that he was the *youngest* son in his family, not the oldest (1 Sam. 16:11). The psalm here indicates how he was placed in a position of preeminence or authority over all other kings. And just as the firstborn of kings is the one who rules over kings, the firstborn of creation (or Jesus) is the one who rules over creation.

. . . It's Praiseworthy to Pray to Jesus

In Revelation 22:13, Jesus says, "I am the Alpha and the Omega, the first and the last, the beginning and the end." Jesus is not one more god in an infinite line of gods nor is he a created being. He is instead eternal like the Father, who is also described as "the Alpha and the Omega, the beginning and the end" (Rev. 21:6). Jesus is the one true God we worship, along with the Father and the Holy Spirit.

But although Mormons pray to the Father, they do not pray to the Son, because from their perspective Jesus is closer to our level of existence than to Heavenly Father's. When they are asked why they don't pray to Jesus, most Mormons will say something like, "Jesus taught his disciples to address their prayers to 'our Father.' He never told us to pray to him."

Yet it doesn't follow that just because Jesus explicitly taught one way to pray that all other ways of prayer are unacceptable. For instance, Mormons give thanks to Heavenly Father even though Jesus never mentioned thanksgiving when he taught us the Lord's Prayer. It seems more likely that Mormons only pray to the Father because they are following a prescription in the Book of Mormon where Jesus says, "[Y]e must always pray unto the Father in my name" (3 Nephi 18:19).

But before he was martyred, St. Stephen prayed directly to the ascended Jesus, saying "Lord Jesus, receive my spirit." And Paul wrote, "[M]ay our Lord Jesus Christ himself and God our Father . . . comfort your hearts and strengthen them in every good work and word" (2 Thess. 2:16–17). Notice that Paul does not ask the Father "in Jesus' name" to comfort believers. He instead petitions *both* the Father and the Son. In his commentary on Thessalonians, Gene Green notes:

> To address prayers to the *Lord Jesus* (so 2 Thess. 3:5,16) in the same breath with God the Father implies a very high Christology. This prayer would be proper only if the apostles held to the divinity of Christ. This point is even clearer in the prayer of 2 Thessalonians 2.16, where the order of the names is reversed.[178]

As I once said to two Mormon missionaries, "I appreciate that you're trying to share your faith, but I love being
a Christian. The reason I could never become a Mormon
is because I would miss the relationship I have with Jesus
Christ. I love praying to Jesus and knowing he isn't 'a god'
but, as the apostle Thomas said, 'My Lord and my God'"
(John 20:28).

The Father in Disguise

On the radio program *Catholic Answers Live* I often appear on shows dedicated to conversations with non-Catholics. Once I appeared on an episode called "Why Aren't You a Christian?" which brought in not just atheists but people from non-Christian religions like Islam and Judaism, as well as people who think they're Christian even though they reject essential Christian doctrines.

"Well, I wanted to call in," began one caller, "because for me Jesus is everything; he's the Lord, he's God, and I'm a Christian even if a lot of people say I'm not." I was puzzled, because this man seemed to affirm one of the key doctrines that divides Christians and non-Christians: the divinity of Christ. But he then talked about how Christians should "baptize in the name of the Jesus" and not in the name of the Father, Son, and Holy Spirit.

So I asked him, "Are you part of the Jesus-only movement?"

He chuckled and replied, "I like to think I'm part of the Jesus-*everything* movement."

This man sounded like a Christian, but he wasn't. He was a member of the Oneness Pentecostal movement, which holds that there is only one God and that Jesus is God, but denies the Trinity. Most people associate the denial of the Trinity with Mormons and Jehovah's Witnesses, but there are over ten million Oneness Pentecostals, which makes them one of the largest quasi-Christian groups in the world.

Jesus told the apostles to "make disciples of all nations, baptizing them in the name of the Father and of the Son and of the Holy Spirit" (Matt. 28:19), but Oneness Pentecostals believe that the "name" of God is *Jesus*. According to them, the terms *Father, Son,* and *Holy Spirit* do not refer to three distinct persons but to three *roles* God plays in our salvation.

This counterfeit Christ is only the "Son of God" in the most idiosyncratic meaning of the term. He is one divine person who acts at various times as the Father who created the world, the Son who redeemed us, and the Holy Spirit who sanctifies us. Oneness theology advocates claim that the only way there can be *one* God who is Father, Son, and Holy Spirit is if everything we know to be God (including the titles of Father, Son, and Holy Spirit) belong to the one divine person we call Jesus Christ.

But how can that be true if . . .

. . . The Father, Son, and Holy Spirit Are Distinct Persons

One of the essential elements of the dogma of the Trinity is that not only are the Father, Son, and Holy Spirit *equal in divinity* to one another, they are also *distinct in identity* from one another. According to the *Catechism*:

The divine persons are really distinct from one another. "God is one but not solitary." "Father," "Son," "Holy Spirit" are not simply names designating modalities of the divine being, for they are really distinct from one another: "He is not the Father who is the Son, nor is the Son he who is the Father, nor is the Holy Spirit he who is the Father or the Son." They are distinct from one another in their relations of origin: "It is the Father who generates, the Son who is begotten, and the Holy Spirit who proceeds." The divine Unity is Triune (254).

One bad analogy for the Trinity compares it to how a man can be a father, brother, and son at the same time, which *does* describe how one person can be three roles, not how one being can be three persons. It actually is a good analogy for the Oneness Pentecostal view of God. Just as my "fatherness" and "sonness" cannot speak to one another, Jesus' human nature (what Oneness proponents call *the Son*) and his divine nature (what they call *the Father*) cannot speak and have relationships with another.

Yet Scripture is full of cases where the Son not only communicates with the Father through prayer, but the Father answers Jesus as an objectively distinct person.

For example, John 12:28 describes Jesus praying to the Father, saying, "Father, glorify thy name." John then tells us that a voice came from heaven, saying, "I have glorified it, and I will glorify it again." Similarly, at both Jesus' baptism and transfiguration the Father speaks in a voice other people can hear, declaring that Jesus is his beloved Son (Matt. 3:17, Matt. 17:5). If Oneness Pentecostalism were true, and God is just one person with three titles or roles, then how could these conversations between persons be happening?

In response, Oneness Pentecostals claim that the Trinity is an illogical doctrine, because it tries to say that three equals one. Their version of Christology, they say, may be a bit of a mystery but no more so than the Trinity. But the Trinity is not illogical or incomprehensible; in fact I have found it to be very helpful in answering common objections to the Christian faith.

For example, once I was having a conversation with a group of atheists about the Trinity and one of them said, "So if Jesus is God, who was he praying to? Himself? Is Jesus his own father?"

I answered by explaining how the term *God* does not always refer to one *person* but it does always refer to one *being* that sustains the universe. In the most general sense of the terms, *being* refers to the fact of existence and *person* refers to the fact of rational relationship. Rocks, plants, and non-human animals exist but they don't have rational relationships. They are beings; not persons. Humans and angels are personal beings but they are limited. God, on the other hand, is unlimited so he is not *a* being but rather *being* itself. God possesses relationships as part of his essence: he is the Father, the Son, and the Holy Spirit, and each of these persons is fully divine and fully distinct from the others.

Saying "Jesus is God" means Jesus is a divine person. Similarly, saying "God is a Trinity" means that this unlimited being exists as three persons.

From that perspective, asking, "Who did Jesus pray to?" poses no challenge to the Christian faith. When Jesus prayed, he was speaking to the other divine person within the Trinity: the Father. But asking, "Who did Jesus pray to?" *does* pose a significant challenge to Oneness Pentecostals. In Scripture, clearly Jesus is praying to the Father not as a separate nature (how do you pray to a nature?) but as a distinct person.

. . . The First Christians Rejected Oneness Theology

Oneness Pentecostals often like to say that their beliefs are apostolic and that trinitarian doctrine was a later corruption. But even by the early second century, Justin Martyr was teaching that the Son and Father are distinct persons. He cites Genesis 1:26 ("Let us make man in our image") to show that "we can indisputably learn that [God] conversed with some one who was numerically distinct from himself, and also a rational being."[179] He also declares, "He who is said to have appeared to Abraham, and to Jacob, and to Moses, and who is called God, is distinct from him who made all things—numerically, I mean, not [distinct] in will."[180]

Not only did the first Christians believe in the Trinity and not espouse Oneness theology; they explicitly rejected this kind of heresy.

In the third century, heretics like Praxeas and Sabellius advocated a version of Oneness theology called *modalism* (though Praxeas later recanted of this heresy). Pope Dionysius and several regional councils condemned these men's errors and early Christian writers refuted their arguments.[181] In the early fifth century, St. Augustine plainly said that "he who is the Son is not the Father; and the Holy Spirit is neither the Father nor the Son."[182]

Some Oneness Pentecostals cite John 10:30 as evidence that Jesus and the Father are the same person, because Jesus said, "I and the Father are one." Ancient heretics also cited this verse but, as we saw in our discussion of Chopra's "guru Jesus," it is erroneous to use it as evidence that there is no distinction between Jesus and the Father. The verb in this verse (*esmen*) is in first-person plural case, so the text literally says, "I and the Father, [*we*] are one."

Similar language elsewhere in Scripture also argues against the Oneness interpretation. When Genesis 2:24 says a husband and wife become "one flesh" in marriage, that doesn't mean they become the same person. It means a special unity exists in their bodies through the marital act. In John 17:21, Jesus prays that all believers may "be one; even as thou, Father, art in me, and I in thee." Just as Jesus is not praying for all believers to become one person, he is not declaring the Father and himself to be one person, either.

In John 10:30, Jesus speaks of the special unity of love, purpose, and divine nature that only exists between him and the Father. The early Christian writer Tertullian said this verse "does not imply singularity of number, but unity of essence, likeness, conjunction, affection on the Father's part, who loves the Son, and submission on the Son's, who obeys the Father's will."[183] In other words, Jesus is proclaiming that he is just as divine as the Father, not that he *is* the Father.

Finally, the early Church's rejection of Oneness theology is evident in its use of the trinitarian baptismal formula. Oneness Pentecostals reject it, arguing that in the book of Acts no one is baptized with it and several verses command baptism to be done "in the name of the Lord" or "in the name of Jesus Christ."

But the Church never took these verses to be baptismal formulas. The evidence from history shows that the early Church understood the baptismal formula as referring to three distinct persons of the Trinity. In the second century, Justin Martyr noted that converts are baptized "in the name of God, the Father and Lord of the universe, and of our Savior Jesus Christ, and of the Holy Spirit."[184] A first-century catechism called the *Didache* also contains instructions for baptism that contradict the "in Jesus' name" formula as well as the Oneness Pentecostal belief that baptism is only valid when done through full submersion:

> And concerning baptism, baptize this way: Having first said all these things, baptize into the name of the Father, and of the Son, and of the Holy Spirit, in living water [running water]. But if you have not living water, baptize into other water; and if you can not in cold, in warm. But if you have not either, pour out water thrice upon the head into the name of Father and Son and Holy Spirit. (14)

. . . The Son Existed Before the Incarnation

Oneness Pentecostals try to explain Jesus' prayers to the Father as communication between his human and divine natures. Even if we granted such an abnormal view of natures, the problem of communication between the Father and Son doesn't go away. Oneness advocates belief that God did not become the Son until the Incarnation, but what about Scripture verses that distinguish the Father and the Son *before* that time?

For example, John the Baptist said of Jesus, "After me comes a man who ranks before me, for he was before me" (John 1:30). Jesus was conceived several months after John was conceived, so this means that the person of Jesus Christ existed before the Incarnation. This is also confirmed by Jesus' declaration that he had "come down from heaven not to do my own will, but the will of him who sent me" (John 6:38).[185] Oneness advocates might respond by saying Jesus existed before his conception as a plan in the Father's mind. But this contradicts what St. Paul tells us in the great *kenosis* or "emptying" hymn in his letter to the Philippians.

After describing self-serving preachers he had to deal with, Paul encourages the Philippians to be humble and act with one another's best interests at heart. He writes, "Have this mind among yourselves, which was in Christ Jesus, who, though he was in the form of God, did not count equality with God a thing to be grasped, but emptied himself, taking the form of a servant, being born in the likeness of men" (Phil. 2:5–7).

Paul cannot be referring to Jesus' existing as a "plan" or "wisdom" in the Father's mind because he is speaking of the preexistent Christ as someone who did not cling to divinity but voluntarily relinquished it for our sake. Plans and wisdom can't be models of humility for us to imitate—only persons can do that.

Finally, the very first verse of John's Gospel declares, "In the beginning was the Word, and the Word was with God, and the Word was God." The Greek word translated "with" in this verse is *pros*, which has a personal connotation and usually refers to *facing toward* someone else. Greek Grammarian A.T. Robertson writes, "*Pros* with the accusative presents a plane of equality and intimacy, face to face with each other."[186]

This means the Word was not a plan in the Father's mind but a person who, as Jesus tells us, was sent by the Father and shared glory with him before the creation of the world. This can be seen when Jesus petitioned the Father, "[G]lorify thou me in thy own presence with the glory *which I had with thee* before the world was made" (John 17:5, emphasis added). Mark McNeil, who converted to Catholicism from Oneness Pentecostalism, provides an apt summary of how the plain meaning of Scripture refutes the idea that Jesus and the Father are the same person:

> The Greek preposition translated "with" in 17:5 is *para*. The word simply means one is *alongside* another. Since

the Son is addressing the Father and refers to the glory
he shared *with* the Father before creation, it is most natural to draw the conclusion that the personal relationship
expressed in that moment of time refers to a relationship
that is eternal.[187]

Some Oneness advocates may ask, "What's the big deal?
What does it matter if we believe God is 'three in one' or
'one in three'?" But the Trinity and the Incarnation are not
abstract, peripheral issues of theology. The *Catechism* says
the Trinity is the central mystery of our faith (234) and the
Incarnation is the distinctive sign of Christian faith (463). A
person who misunderstands either risks placing their salvation in a false Christ incapable of saving anyone.

More troubling, the Oneness advocate's confused understanding of Christ's natures leads to a deficient Christology. As Oneness theology proponent David Bernard writes,
"One way to explain the human and divine in Christ is to
say he was God living in a human house."[188]

If Jesus were just a divine person wearing a human costume that he communicated with (like Tony Stark in his
Iron Man suit) then we couldn't really say that the Word
became flesh and dwelt among us (John 1:14). Christ's death
on the cross would just be the Father's release from a human body instead of a sacrifice of love the Son offers to the
Father for the atonement of our sins. That's why Tertullian
bluntly told his modalist opponents that they were "con-
tending against the definite purpose of the gospel. For these
things certainly are not written that you may believe that
Jesus Christ is the Father, but the Son" [John 20:31].[189]

Finally, just as the fundamental revelation that there is
only one God cannot accommodate the henotheism of
Mormon theology, the gospel's foundational proclamation

that God loved the world and *gave his Son* to save it (John 3:16) cannot accommodate Oneness theology. Such a distortion of the Faith would undermine the glorious truth that God is love (1 John 4:18) and that this eternal love is fully revealed by the love that is shared between the Father, Son, and Holy Spirit.

COUNTERFEITS
from
Ideologues

13

"Gay-Affirming" Savior

Whenever the topic of homosexuality and the Bible comes up, it doesn't take long before someone says, "Jesus never said anything about homosexuality!" In a 2012 interview, former president Jimmy Carter essentially did that when he said:

> Homosexuality was well known in the ancient world, well before Christ was born, and Jesus never said a word about homosexuality. In all of his teachings about multiple things—he never said that gay people should be condemned. I personally think it is very fine for gay people to be married in civil ceremonies.[190]

Some go a step further and claim that Jesus *affirmed* homosexual behavior. For example, one pro-gay Christian website claims that the centurion who sought Jesus' help to heal his servant in Matthew, chapter eight, was actually in a sexual relationship with that servant. Their primary evidence for this comes from the centurion's use of the term *pais* to describe the servant, which they say refers to a male lover. From this they conclude, "Jesus restores a gay relationship by a miracle of healing and then holds up a gay man as an example of faith for all to follow."[191]

Regardless of what Jesus said or didn't say about homosexuality in the Bible, this counterfeit Christ would never condemn homosexual behavior today. He would instead affirm such behavior as part of healthy relationships that are morally equivalent to marital love between men and women.

But how can that be true if . . .

. . . Jesus Never Affirmed Homosexual Behavior

Just because Jesus healed someone it doesn't follow that Jesus affirmed everything that person did. When Jesus healed ten lepers, only one of them returned to give God glory for his healing, but that doesn't mean Jesus endorsed the religious laxity of the other nine (Luke 17:11–19)

Similarly, even if the centurion and his servant had a sexual relationship, does it follow that Jesus' miracle meant he affirmed the practice of older men purchasing younger male sex slaves? I doubt the revisionist critic would say, "Jesus restores a master-slave relationship by a miracle of healing and then holds up a slave owner as an example of faith for all to follow."

Throughout the Gospels, Jesus shows compassion to people *in spite of* their sins, and his healings and deliverance from harm are invitations to further spiritual salvation. For example, Jesus saved the woman caught in adultery from being executed, not so that she could return to her sinful ways, but so that she could *repent* of them. That's why he said to her, "do not sin again" (John 8:11).

That said, there is no evidence that the centurion and his slave actually were involved in a sexual relationship. New Testament professor John Byron writes:

The Greek noun *pais* is used in the New Testament twenty-four times and has a range of meanings that include "adolescent," "child," and "servant." [In the Greek Old Testament] it appears numerous times and it always refers to a "servant." There are no occurrences of the term anywhere in the Bible that can be interpreted [as] referring to the junior partner in a homosexual relationship.[192]

Other attempts to tease out of Scripture hidden pro-homosexual meanings are similarly dubious. It's no wonder, then, that the arguments for a "gay-affirming" Jesus are usually arguments from silence—arguments based on what Jesus did *not* say. They claim, in so many words, that since Jesus never condemned homosexuality he must not have seen anything wrong with it.

But we actually don't know if Jesus *never* said anything about homosexuality, because Jesus said many things that are not recorded in Scripture (John 21:25).

For example, when Paul was in Ephesus he spoke to the elders of the churches there, exhorting them to provide for the needs of the Church in Jerusalem. He then said to them, "In all things I have shown you that by so toiling one must help the weak, remembering the words of the Lord Jesus, how he said, 'It is more blessed to give than to receive'" (Acts 20:35).

Even though Paul relates this saying of Jesus in a way that suggests it's well known, nowhere is it recorded in the Gospels. This is one indication of how some of Jesus' teachings were not written in the accounts of his life but were passed down through oral means (what Catholics call Sacred Tradition).

Since there is an unbroken tradition of Christians condemning same-sex behavior from the beginning of the Church's history, we can safely conclude this tradition comes from Jesus and the apostles. Indeed, it would be downright bizarre if Jesus approved of homosexual behavior only to have all his followers teach the opposite—including Paul, whom Jesus chose as an apostle and inspired author but who clearly condemns homosexual behavior in his own writings (Rom. 1:26–28, 1 Cor. 6:9–10, 1 Tim. 1:10).[193]

The Episcopalian bishop Gene Robinson is in a legal marriage with another man, yet when it comes to Jesus' silence on homosexuality he admits, "One cannot extrapolate affirmation of such relationships from that silence." Robinson instead claims that all "we can safely and responsibly conclude from Jesus' silence is that he was silent on the issue."[194] I wonder if Robinson would likewise say that "all we can safely and responsibly conclude from Jesus' silence on polygamy, incest, bestiality, idolatry, and child sacrifice is that he was silent on those issues."

He likely wouldn't, because Jesus' affirmation of the Old Testament's prohibitions on, for example, murder, show he would never have supported child sacrifice and so it is an absurd question to ask. Likewise, Jesus' affirmation of the Old Testament's prohibitions on sexual immorality show he would never have supported sexual activity between people of the same sex, or any kind of behavior that violated the universal moral law.

. . . Jesus Upheld the Old Testament's Moral Laws

The idea that Jesus upheld the Old Testament might surprise people who believe he simply did away with it. But Jesus said, "Think not that I have come to abolish the law and the prophets; I have come not to abolish them but to fulfill them" (Matt. 5:17). In some cases this fulfillment took the form of *strengthening* these laws, such as when Jesus commanded the love of both neighbor *and* enemy (Matt. 5:43–44), condemned lust as a type of adultery (Matt. 5:27–28), and condemned anger as a type of murder (1 John 3:15, Matt. 5:21–22).

In other cases, fulfillment involved replacing these laws by revealing the deeper lessons they were designed to teach God's people (CCC 582). One example of this was when Jesus did away with the Old Testament's dietary laws, saying it is the evil thoughts from *within* that defile us rather than the foods we consume (Mark 7:14–23). But were the Old Testament's prohibitions on homosexual behavior ritual laws that were replaced, or moral laws that were not just retained but expanded in order to achieve a moral ideal?

Leviticus 18:22 reads, "You shall not lie with a male as with a woman; it is an abomination." This verse is sandwiched between verses clearly containing moral laws, not ceremonial ones. Verse twenty condemns adultery, verse twenty-one condemns child sacrifice, and verse twenty-three condemns bestiality.[195] Leviticus 18:24–25 also makes it clear that actions like adultery, bestiality, and same-sex relations were part of the moral law that applied to non-Jews as well, because God had previously judged other pagan nations for engaging in these "defilements."

Furthermore, unlike with idolatry, murder, adultery, or breaking the Sabbath, the Old Testament never prescribes the death penalty for violating mere ceremonial laws. Leviticus 20 mandates exile for someone who becomes unclean by having sex with a menstruating woman; but it prescribes death for adultery, bestiality, and same-sex behavior, all of which fall under the unchanging moral law. That today we don't usually enforce such harsh penalties for those acts doesn't mean they're not serious violations of the moral law.

Some proponents of the gay-affirming Jesus look for textual loopholes in these verses. Revisionist scholar John Boswell, for example, claims that the Hebrew word translated "abomination" in Leviticus 18:22, *toevah*, is merely referring to ritual impurities like the eating of unclean foods and not grave moral evils.[196] But although *toevah* can refer to this, in the rest of the Old Testament it usually refers to grave moral evils like child sacrifice (Deut. 12:31), adultery (Ezek. 18:10–13), and murder (Prov. 6:17).[197] And in Ezekiel 16:50 it refers to the sins of the people of Sodom, which included homosexual intercourse.[198]

Boswell and other revisionists also claim that the passages in Leviticus only refer to homosexual acts in the context of prostitution or pagan temple sacrifices—not consensual, loving same-sex relationships, which he claims were unheard of at the time.[199] But ancient Mesopotamian texts like the *Almanac of Incantations* do describe consensual, same-sex relationships, so it was not an unheard-of concept in the ancient world. And there is a specific Hebrew word for temple prostitutes (*qadeshim*), but Leviticus 18 doesn't use it. So this interpretation fails.[200]

If the author of Leviticus were alive today, he would say that the prohibitions on same-sex intercourse apply not just to Jews who were given the Mosaic Law but also to all people who can understand the natural law through their moral conscience. That is why Paul cited the immorality of homosexual behavior as an example of God's judging how the Gentiles responded to the revelation he gave them through their own moral consciences (Rom. 1:24–28).

Jesus told the young scholar of the law that in order to be saved he had to keep the Ten Commandments (Matt. 19:17); this means Jesus would not have affirmed *any* immoral sexual behavior, be it adultery, fornication, or sodomy, that violated the sixth commandment. Robert Gagnon makes the point well:

> Jesus took sexual sin very seriously—in some respects more seriously than the prevailing culture in first-century Palestine. He regarded all sexual activity (thoughts and deeds) outside of lifelong marriage to one person of the opposite sex as capable of jeopardizing one's entrance into the kingdom of God. In relation to our own cultural context, Jesus' views on sex represent on the whole a staunchly conservative position. Those who find in the Gospels a Jesus who is a prophet of tolerance, who forgives and accepts all (except, perhaps, the intolerant), regardless of behavioral change, have distorted the historical reality.[201]

. . . Jesus Condemned "Consensual" Sexual Immorality

In his book *Radical Love: Introduction to Queer Theology*, Patrick Cheng claims, "Radical love is ultimately about *love* [emphasis in original], which, as St. Paul teaches us, is patient and kind, and not envious, boastful, arrogant, or rude. As such, radical love is premised upon safe, sane, and consensual behavior."[202] This language jibes with a prevailing modern sexual ethic that emphasizes consent and taking precautions against disease and pregnancy.

But the real Jesus condemned at least one sexual behavior that modern people usually consider to be "safe, sane, and consensual"—remarriage after divorce. And because Jesus did that, we know what principles grounded his sexual ethics; and through those principles we can safely conclude what Jesus believed about the morality of homosexual behavior.

In the first century there was dispute among Jews over when divorce was permissible. Deuteronomy 24:1 allowed a husband to divorce his wife if "she finds no favor in his eyes because he has found some indecency in her." The two most important figures in this debate were the rabbis Hillel and Shammai, who founded two opposing schools of thought among the Pharisees. The followers of Hillel believed divorce could be justified for virtually any reason or "indecency," including a wife accidentally ruining her husband's dinner. The followers of Shammai, on the other hand, said divorce was only permissible in the case of adultery.[203]

The Pharisees brought this debate to Jesus by asking him, "Is it lawful to divorce one's wife for any cause?" (Matt. 19:3). Instead of siding with one group of Pharisees over another, Jesus answered them by going back to a more fundamental law:

> Have you not read that he who made them from the beginning made them male and female, and said, "For this reason a man shall leave his father and mother and be joined to his wife, and the two shall become one?" So they are no longer two but one. What therefore God has joined together, let not man put asunder (Matt. 19:4–6).

In this answer, Jesus presented an interpretation of the moral law that was stricter than the strictest of the Pharisees: *no sin* could dissolve the marriage bond God created. In response, the Pharisees brought up Deuteronomy's provision for divorce, to which Jesus replied, "For your hardness of heart Moses allowed you to divorce your wives, but from the beginning it was not so. And I say to you: whoever divorces his wife, except for unchastity, and marries another, commits adultery; and he who marries a divorced woman, commits adultery" (Matt. 19:8–9).

There is a debate over what Jesus meant by "except for unchastity."

This can't refer simply to adultery because the Greek word for adultery (*moicheia*) is not used but rather the Greek word for general sexual immorality (*porneia*). Some scholars think Jesus could be referring to an invalid marriage between relatives that can be dissolved because of its intrinsically sinful nature. Or, he might mean that a man can remarry if he divorced his wife on suspicion of sexual impropriety during the period between the marriage ceremony and the marriage's consummation (which could be as long as a year in the ancient world). In fact, this is what St. Joseph briefly considered before God reassured him in a dream that Mary had conceived by the Holy Spirit.[204]

Whatever it means, the parallel passage in Mark leaves no doubt as to Jesus' teaching about remarriage after divorce: "Whoever divorces his wife and marries another, commits adultery against her; and if she divorces her husband and marries another, she commits adultery" (Mark 10:11–12).

Some people try to diffuse the force of Jesus' teaching by saying that he was trying to be *ironic*, since wives weren't allowed to divorce their husbands. But although wife-initiated divorce was rare in the ancient near East, it was not unheard-of, either. Exodus 21:10–11 describes how a slave married to her master can leave him without paying any sort of penalty if he fails to provide for her needs, including "marital rights."

A second-century divorce certificate (in Hebrew a *get*) addressed to a husband from his wife was even discovered in the Judean desert in 1951.[205] According to David Instone-Brewer in his study on divorce and remarriage in the Bible, "Normally women would not write a divorce certificate such as this one, but they would ask a court to persuade their husbands to write one. Perhaps this nonrabbinic practice was influenced by the Greco-Roman world where women could initiate divorce, as wealthy Jewish women in the first century are known to have done."[206]

Jesus did not care if second marriages were, as Cheng says, "safe, sane, and consensual." He also didn't quibble with his opponents about possible exceptions in the Deuteronomic code. He instead went all the way back to creation itself and rooted the morality of sex in the permanent, life-giving nature of marital love that God designed in our own bodies (Gen. 2:23–25). If Jesus condemned what critics would today call "harmless thoughts" (lust) and "finding your soulmate" (adulterous remarriage) because these violated that permanent design found in the one-flesh union that only exists between a man and woman, there is no way he would affirm the use of our sexual organs outside of that context within same-sex relationships.

Jesus did not teach that what mattered most is finding happiness through our bodily desires. After saying lust was a kind of adultery, Jesus advised his hearers, "If your right eye causes you to sin, pluck it out and throw it away; it is better that you lose one of your members than that your whole body be thrown into hell" (Matt. 5:30). Jesus' hyperbole is not a recommendation of mutilation but of *mortification*: the disciplined subjection of our bodily desires so that they serve our heavenly destiny.

Our bodily desires are strong, but the grace of God is stronger, so anyone who struggles with disordered sexual attractions (no matter their object) should not give into despair and hopelessness. We all feel the "war in our bodies" (Rom. 7:23) tempting us to reject God's will for us, and so we should look to Christ, not as a heartless judge but as a compassionate savior. He allowed his body to be mocked, abused, scourged, and crucified so that our bodily desires would not condemn our eternal souls.

14

Socialist Liberator

In the Stern Dining Hall of Stanford University there is a painting by Antonio Burciaga called *The Last Supper of Chicano Heroes*. It's an *homage* to Da Vinci's *Last Supper* but with Hispanic heroes in place of Jesus and the apostles. The mural has generated controversy because of its depiction of socialist revolutionary Che Guevara in the place of Jesus Christ. One outraged student wrote in a Stanford newspaper, "Che Guevara was a butcher and a tyrant. It is utterly disgusting, offensive, and ignorant for Casa Zapata to deify him on its walls."[207]

But many people think it's entirely appropriate to compare Che to Jesus because both men were "socialists" who liberated the poor. In her popular book *Nickel and Dimed: On (Not) Getting By in America,* Barbara Ehrenreich says Jesus was a "wine-guzzling vagrant and precocious socialist" whose inconvenient message about helping the poor the Church tries to suppress.[208] In 2015, Bolivian president and head of the Movement for Socialist party Evo Morales gifted Pope Francis with a "Communist crucifix." It depicted Christ crucified on a hammer and sickle (the symbol of the Communist party in the Soviet Union) in an effort to show that socialism and Christianity are compatible with one another.[209]

Pope Pius XI said "no one can be at the same time a good
Catholic and a true socialist,"[210] but this counterfeit Christ
says the exact opposite: the *only* good Catholics are true socialists. If you really cared about the poor, if you really accepted the call of Christ to care for the "least among us"
(Matt. 25:40) then you would support socialist policies to
eliminate poverty.

But how can that be true if . . .
. . . Jesus Did Not Preach Socialist Policies

If you define a socialist as "a person who wants to help the
poor," then Jesus was a socialist—but then so is almost everyone else. What makes someone a socialist is not his desire
to help the poor but his belief about what kind of economy
provides the most benefit to the poor.

Capitalism, for example, is defined in terms of private
ownership of the means to produce goods and services.
Usually, this kind of capitalism takes place within a "market
economy" that allows for the free exchange of goods and
services as a means to create profit. Capitalists believe that
this voluntary series of exchanges makes everyone in the
economy wealthier and that this is the most effective way to
lift people out of poverty.

Socialism, on the other hand, refers to the collective
or "social" ownership of the means to produce goods and
services. There are several different kinds of economic
models that have been called socialism, but according to *The
Oxford Companion to Christian Thought*, "By its very nature
[socialism] involves the abolition of private ownership of
capital; bringing the means of production, distribution, and
exchange into public ownership and control is central to
its philosophy."[211] Socialists claim the best way to alleviate

poverty is through a central authority like the government (as opposed to decentralized forces like the market) distributing a society's wealth among its individual members.

If *this* is what is meant by "socialism," then Jesus was not a socialist because Jesus did not seek to abolish the private ownership of capital (like money or natural resources) or the means of production like organized farms and manufacturing technologies. According to economist Lawrence Reed, "The fact is, one can scour the scriptures with a fine-tooth comb and find nary a word from Jesus that endorses the forcible redistribution of wealth by political authorities. None, period."[212]

But even if Jesus didn't preach socialist political *policies,* couldn't we say he preached socialist *values* when it came to individuals? After all, he told the rich man that if he wanted to inherit eternal life he should sell what he had and give it to the poor (Mark 10:21). Doesn't this mean that Jesus wanted the rich to give away all their money to the poor?

It should first be noted that giving away your money to the poor is a *charitable* value rather than a *socialist* one. Jesus' commands for individuals to give alms to the poor (Luke 12:33) did not include whether those individuals should give that money directly to the poor, donate it to charities who serve the poor, or allow the money to be taxed and redistributed though government subsidy programs. Helping the poor is a non-negotiable issue for Christians, but there can be reasonable disagreement among believers over which methods are the best way to reduce poverty.

Furthermore, we must remember that Jesus often used hyperbole when speaking with people in order to underscore the importance of his teachings. When Jesus told the rich man to sell all his possessions, he was not being a "Robin Hood" who wanted to take wealth from a corrupt rich

man and give it back to the deserving poor. We know that
because the man asked Jesus about getting to heaven and
Jesus reminded him that he must keep the commandments.
After the man said he had kept the commandments since his
youth (a point Jesus does not dispute) Mark tells us:

> And Jesus looking upon him loved him, and said to him,
> "You lack one thing; go, sell what you have, and give
> to the poor, and you will have treasure in heaven; and
> come, follow me." At that saying his countenance fell,
> and he went away sorrowful; for he had great possessions
> (10:21–22).

Jesus was calling this man to rise above a minimal obe-
dience to the law and to truly love God above all things,
including material possessions. That's why Jesus said in another sermon, "No one can serve two masters; for either he
will hate the one and love the other, or he will be devoted
to the one and despise the other. You cannot serve God and
mammon [money]" (Matt. 6:24). That Jesus did not expect
every rich person to give away all he owned is evident in his
encounter with a rich man, who made "the right decision"
while in his presence.

When Jesus agreed to dine with the diminutive tax collector Zaccheus, that man said, "Behold, Lord, the half of
my goods I give to the poor; and if I have defrauded any
one of anything, I restore it fourfold" (Luke 19:8). Instead of
saying, "Half isn't good enough! Sell everything and follow
me," Jesus said, "Today salvation has come to this house"
(Luke 19:9).

Zaccheus and other wealthy disciples of Jesus like Joseph
of Arimathea (who could afford an expensive rock tomb for
Jesus' burial) show that it is not impossible for the rich to

inherit the kingdom of God. They can inherit the kingdom through the same grace that is given to everyone else. Jesus put it this way when he was asked about the salvation of not just the rich, but anyone who trusts in his own efforts: "With men this is impossible, but with God all things are possible" (Matt. 19:26).

. . . "Socialist Jesus" Is an Anachronism

Jesus was neither a socialist nor a capitalist because both of these economic systems were not invented until more than a thousand years after his earthly ministry. This also means we can't fully understand Jesus' views on wealth and poverty unless we understand the economy of Jesus' time.

In the ancient world, wealth was like a single delicious pie that grandma made for the whole family. If I take half the pie in a single slice, my siblings would rightfully be angry with me. It's impossible for me to have such a large piece without causing everyone else in the family to have very small pieces (or go without). Economists call this a *zero-sum game*, and it means that the only way I can "win" at the game of eating pie is if other people lose.

In the first century, wealth creation was a zero-sum game. Ordinary people could grow or acquire only enough food to meet their basic needs, and any surplus was shared with relatives or kin who were not so well off. The rich in Jesus' time were seen as hoarders whose excess directly contributed to everyone else's poverty. That's why Jesus condemned the "rich fool" who stored up resources in his barns instead of putting them to use to help others (Luke 12:16–21).

In Jesus' time, the rich acquired their wealth not through the free exchange of goods and services, but almost always by extorting or manipulating the poor through unjust taxation and predatory lending. One ancient Mediterranean proverb said, "Every rich person is a thief or the son of a thief." So when Jesus said, "It is easier for a camel to go through the eye of a needle than for a rich man to enter the kingdom of God" (Matt. 19:24), he was referring to how common it was for the rich to attain their wealth through sinful means.[213]

But today, wealth can be created in moral ways that do not exploit people and we don't have to view wealth as a single pie. It's more like the output of an oven that is capable of making many pies. For example, imagine if a dozen families bring me the ingredients for apple pies and I turn them into whole pies at the cost of one slice per pie. By the end of the day I might have more pie than any of the individual families that came to my bakery, but my "pie wealth" didn't come at their expense. Indeed, it was a byproduct of the very process that gave them their pie in the first place.

But just like in the time of Christ, there is a temptation to love money more than God, so all of us must guard against the sin of greed—not just the wealthy. For example, Luke describes how a person following Jesus said to him, "Teacher, bid my brother divide the inheritance with me." Instead of helping this man "redistribute wealth" Jesus answered him, "Man, who made me a judge or divider over you?" He then said to the crowd following him, "Take heed, and beware of all covetousness; for a man's life does not consist in the abundance of his possessions" (Luke 12:13–15).

. . . Marxism Is Incompatible with Christianity

The most perverse thing about the Communist crucifix that Evo Morales gave to Pope Francis is that Communist regimes like the Soviet Union tried to destroy the Church and murdered millions of Christians in the process.[214] Giving a

"Communist crucifix" to the pope should be as offensive as giving a rabbi a Star of David affixed to a swastika.

Some people claim that Christians can separate the harsh authoritarianism of these Communist regimes from the allegedly beneficial economic policies of socialism. But the evil of socialism is not found solely in the authoritarian suppression that accompanies it in Communist regimes. It arises first from its rejection of a person's right to own private property and to dispose of it as he chooses. According to the textbook *Essentials of Sociology*:

> The terms socialism and Communism are often used more or less interchangeably. . . . From a Marxian perspective, socialism can be seen as a historical stage following communism. It involves the effort by society to plan and organize production consciously and rationally so that all members of society benefit from it.[215]

In fact, an entire field called *liberation theology* attempts to combine Jesus' concern for the poor with the socialist thought of Karl Marx. One of these ideas is the Marxist principle of "class struggle," or the claim that the upper classes always cause others to be poor and so the lower classes must seize political power and establish their own "dictatorship" with the goal of creating a "class-less society."

In Gustavo Gutierrez's classic text *A Theology of Liberation* he writes, "The class struggle is a fact that Christians cannot dodge and in the face of which the demands of the gospel must be clearly stated."[216]

In 1984 the Congregation for the Doctrine of the Faith (CDF) released its *Instruction on Certain Aspects of the "Theology of Liberation."* The CDF agreed that Christians have a special obligation to help the poor (this idea is known in

Catholic social teaching as the "preferential option for the poor") and they should not tolerate unjust conditions that create widespread poverty. But the document goes on to quote Pope Paul VI, who said it was "dangerous" to "enter into the practice of class-struggle and of its Marxist interpretation while failing to see the kind of totalitarian society to which this process slowly leads" (7).

In his critique of liberation theology, Jean Galot says:

> [A] program for a class struggle is completely foreign to Jesus' intentions and mentality. . . . The class struggle implies a clear-cut exclusion directed against a certain social class. It assumes that the "social sin" of exploitation and injustice is concentrated in this class and hence that this class must be eliminated. In light of the gospel, we cannot accept such a struggle.[217]

The CDF rebuked the idea that evil can be localized "principally or uniquely in bad social, political, or economic 'structures' as though all other evils came from them so that the creation of the 'new man' would depend on the establishment of different economic and socio-political structures" (15). In response, liberation theologians like Juan Segundo blasted the 1984 instruction as (in the words of political theory scholar Paul Sigmund) "a general attack on Enlightenment humanism and modern thought, aimed at reestablishing an other-worldly and transcendentalist religion."[218]

Of course, Jesus said the kingdom of God is literally "not of this world" (John 18:36) and that the poor are blessed because they will be admitted to this kingdom (Luke 6:20). In a 2014 press conference on liberation theology (with Segundo in attendance) Cardinal Gerhard Mueller said that "the Church speaks about poor in a very different way than the Communists do. Christians do not dream of an earthly paradise, and the Communists always blamed us that the Church only deals with heaven."[219]

Christians don't treat heaven as "pie in the sky when you die," or something to distract us from suffering on earth.[220] But we also recognize that we are fallen creatures who cannot create a "heaven on earth" through the adoption of a specific political regime or economic system.

When Jesus spoke in the synagogue, he said that the words of Isaiah promising a deliverer who would "proclaim good news to the poor," "release the captives," "set at liberty those who are oppressed," and "proclaim the acceptable year of the Lord" had been fulfilled in their presence (Luke 4:18). The year he was talking about was the Jubilee, which was celebrated every fifty years in Israel and involved the cancellation of debts, the freeing of slaves, and most importantly, the remission of sins that were seen as the ultimate debt we could never pay.

Jesus' promise to "set us free" does include freedom from temporal evils and oppression. But this promise finds its fullest expression in being Jesus' disciples and knowing the truth about his saving mission and how it sets us free from the slavery of sin (John 8:31–34).

In the year 2000, the Catholic Church declared its own Jubilee and celebrated genuine liberation through Christ saying, "Jesus comes to offer us a salvation which, although primarily a liberation from sin, also involves the totality of our being with its deepest needs and aspirations. Christ frees us from this burden and threat and opens the way to the complete fulfillment of our destiny."[221]

Flawed & Failed Prophet

Aut deus aut homo malus, or in English, "Either God or a bad man." That's the Latin summary of C.S. Lewis's famous "trilemma" argument we discussed in chapter one. If Jesus really said what the Bible records, then he must be a lunatic, a liar, or the Lord—and if he isn't the first two then he must be the third.

But, what if Jesus' own words prove that he *was* either a lunatic or a liar (and therefore a bad man)?

Take his seemingly failed prophecies, for example. Lewis admitted that Matthew 24:34 is "the most embarrassing verse in the Bible" because, after apocalyptically describing how "the stars will fall from heaven" (among other cosmic calamities), Jesus said, "Truly, I say to you, this generation will not pass away till all these things take place."[222] Former Christian apologist-turned atheist John Loftus says of Jesus' allegedly imminent predictions of the end of the world, "Either Jesus was a failed prophet or the New Testament isn't even somewhat reliable. Either way, this falsifies Christianity."[223]

Other critics say that Jesus' so-called moral advice actually proves he was not worthy of our worship. Stephanie Coontz claims that "a radical antifamily ideology permeates Christ's teaching. . . . leave your parents, siblings, and spouse to follow me—even if you must 'hate' them in order to leave [Luke 14:26]. Do not even stop, Jesus tells one follower, to bury your own father [Matt. 8:22]."[224] Popular Hollywood movies like *The Last Temptation of Christ* depict Jesus as a sinner who was unsure of his divine mission; recent surveys show half of young people (and a third of Christian teens) believe Jesus was not perfect and could have sinned.[225]

So if Jesus gives immoral advice and incorrect teachings about the future, then doesn't it follow that he was a charlatan or a crazy person, and not our Lord and Savior after all?

But how can that be true if . . .

. . . Jesus Was Prophesying the Destruction of Jerusalem

Biblical prophecy has more than one kind of fulfillment, and often requires understanding both of history and of Hebrew idioms. The Bible's descriptions of cosmic destruction, for example, can refer both to the Second Coming and the end of the world, but they can also refer to other kinds of destruction that, to the people of the time, was "the end of their world." For example, in Isaiah 13:10–11 God says, "For the stars of the heavens and their constellations will not give their light; the sun will be dark at its rising and the moon will not shed its light. I will punish the world for its evil, and the wicked for their iniquity."

However, this is not a prophecy about the destruction of the entire world but the destruction of the Babylonian Empire. Likewise, when Jesus spoke of "the stars falling" (an idiom that refers to the downfall of political powers) or "the coming of his kingdom in power" he may have been referring to similar localized events. For example, when Jesus said, "There are some standing here who will not taste death before they see the Son of Man coming in his kingdom" (Mark 9:1), this may refer to the disciples who would see him come in glory during his Transfiguration, which happened just six days after he uttered this teaching.[226]

It may also refer to Jesus' "coming in power" during the cataclysmic destruction of Jerusalem in A.D. 70, which would be similar to Isaiah 19's description of how God "came to Egypt" in judgment of that nation through an Assyrian attack on it. We know that part of Jesus' message was about Jerusalem's destruction because just before he described several apocalyptic signs he pointed to the temple and said, "There will not be left here one stone upon another, that will not be thrown down" (Matt. 24:2).[227] According to Fr. William Most:

> The coming is best understood within the common scriptural concept of *visitation,* God intervening to help, to save, to punish. The intervention of Jesus, his coming, probably refers to the wars of A.D. 66–70 and the fall of Jerusalem, which put an end to the Jewish persecutions before the disciples ran out of places in which to preach.[228]

But what about Jesus' declaration that the generation hearing his words would see how "the stars will fall" (24:29) as well as "the Son of Man coming on the clouds of heaven with power and great glory" (24:30)? How can those things refer to the destruction of the temple? They can if we consider that first-century Jews viewed the temple in Jerusalem as a representation of the universe itself.

In his history of the Jewish War, Josephus said that within the temple "the seven lamps signified the seven planets" and "the twelve loaves that were upon the table signified the circle of the zodiac."[229] The temple's veil that guarded the Holy of Holies "had also embroidered upon it all that was mystical in the heavens."[230] According to religion scholar Douglas R. Edwards, "The temple curtain is depicted as various aspects of the cosmos and symbolizes that the temple, and in particular, the Holy of Holies embody the very fabric of their existence."[231]

Therefore, the destruction of artifacts within the temple bearing images of the stars and planets was seen as a kind of destruction of those things, and not as just of "another building" destroyed during the great siege. In that respect, Jesus was speaking about the end of *a* world (or the Jewish worship of God in a specific place like the temple) but not the end of *the* world.

. . . Jesus Taught in a Different Historical Context

Because Jesus lived in a foreign culture thousands of years ago, it can be easy to misunderstand things he said. The destruction of Jerusalem, for example, makes another appearance in the oft-misunderstood episode of Jesus cursing the fig tree. Matthew describes the event:

> In the morning, as [Jesus] was returning to the city, he was hungry. And seeing a fig tree by the wayside he went to it, and found nothing on it but leaves only. And he said to it, "May no fruit ever come from you again!" And the fig tree withered at once (Matt. 21:18–20).

Dan Barker says of this incident, "Is it kind or rational to destroy a plant that happens to be out of season when you are hungry? Is such behavior indicative of mental health?"[232]

But Jesus wasn't throwing a temper tantrum because he was hungry.

Rabbis often used fig trees to teach lessons, and ancient Roman sources reveal how "the fig tree stands out as a tree that produces fruit before leaves . . . the presence of leaves makes intelligible to Mark's readers why Jesus went in search of something to eat."[233] Just as this tree had outward signs of fruit but no real fruit, so too did the hypocritical religious leaders of Jerusalem have all the outward signs of piety even though their hearts were far from God (Matt. 15:8), and so they bore no spiritual fruit and would eventually be "cut down" (John 15:2).

The fact that Mark and Matthew describe Jesus driving the money-changers out of the temple in the middle of their story about the withered fig tree story shows that this was the larger issue to which Jesus was referring. The presence of a barren tree hearkens back to descriptions of Israel being barren and failing to produce spiritual fruit for God (Jer. 8:13) and alludes to Jesus' other parable about a barren fig tree that is cut down because of its fruitlessness (Luke 13:6–9). In his commentary on this passage, Mark Keown writes, "In cursing the fig tree, Jesus is not showing a vindictive destructive attitude to God's creation, or a fit of anger from an overly hungry (hangry) man, but is visually enacting the forthcoming destruction of Israel because of her failure to yield to God."[234]

If we didn't know these subtle details about religious and even botanical life in ancient Israel, we could easily be misled and think Jesus was eccentric at best or unhinged at worst.

Another example where cultural details that are far removed from us can make all the difference is Jesus' assertion, "If any one comes to me and does not hate his own father and mother and wife and children and brothers and sisters, yes, and even his own life, he cannot be my disciple" (Luke 14:26).

Does Jesus really want us to hate our families and even ourselves?

Remember that words often have meaning in popular usage that goes beyond the dictionary definition. For example, saying, "Don't be a hater" to someone who merely doesn't like my favorite kind of music is an invitation for him to have an open mind. It is not a command for him to abandon a malicious attitude.

Similarly, according to ancient Jewish idiom, to "hate" someone could just mean "to love him less than others," and not refer to malice or anger. This can be seen with the patriarch Jacob, who was married to Rachel and Leah, the daughters of his uncle Laban. Genesis 29:30–31 says, "So Jacob went in to Rachel also, and he loved Rachel more than Leah, and served Laban for another seven years. When the Lord saw that Leah was hated, he opened her womb; but Rachel was barren."

Jacob didn't *hate* Leah. He just loved her less than Rachel, who was the woman he originally wanted to marry before his uncle tricked him into marrying Leah. (For more on this ancient Mediterranean drama, see Genesis 29–30.)

We should remember that as a good Jew, Jesus obeyed all of the Ten Commandments, including the fourth: "Honor your father and mother." He even criticized the Pharisees for shirking this responsibility (Mark 7:9–13). But Jesus knew that our love for God must come first, and that nothing on earth, even the people closest to us, can be more important than that love for him. Matthew 10:37–38 describes the same saying, but rephrases it slightly so that the meaning is easier to discern: "Whoever loves father or mother more than me is not worthy of me, and whoever loves son or daughter more than me is not worthy of me; and whoever does not take up his cross and follow after me is not worthy of me."

This also explains Jesus' seemingly harsh reply to a man who wanted to follow Jesus but asked him, "Lord, let me first go and bury my father." Jesus told him, "Follow me, and leave the dead to bury their own dead" (Matt. 8:22). This may seem harsh, but that's because we assume the man's father had just died. But when someone died in ancient Israel, the law commanded that he be buried immediately (Deut. 21:23). If this young man's father had just died, he would not be with Jesus, but with his family before embarking on a funeral procession to the family tomb.

So what did the man mean? New Testament scholar Craig Keener informs us, "[F]ather and son might wish to be together before the father died, and Semitic idioms in other languages might suggest that 'I must first bury my father' could function as a request to wait until one's father dies—perhaps for years."[235]

In this case, Jesus' call to discipleship meant leaving everything behind, including family ties, for the sake of proclaiming the gospel—not leaving your father's corpse unburied.

There are many other examples of Jesus saying things that, to our modern ears, may seem absurd or even impossible. But if Jesus is God and God can't give bad advice, it follows that Jesus' hard sayings are only "hard" because we don't understand what he meant—not because Jesus made a mistake. In fact, this brings us to the most obvious reason why Jesus could not have been a failed prophet or a flawed moral teacher: he is God incarnate and so failure and sin are impossible for him.

. . . For Jesus, Sin and Ignorance Are Impossible

Some modern critics may try to explain Jesus' hard sayings or his allegedly failed prophecies as byproducts of his human nature. Even if Jesus was the Son of God, Jesus was still a human being, and so perhaps he was ignorant of his divine identity?

This theme is common in Hollywood productions that depict Jesus as being fearful and unsure of his mission. But the *Catechism* says, "By its union to the divine wisdom in the person of the Word incarnate, Christ enjoyed in his human knowledge the fullness of understanding of the eternal plans he had come to reveal" (CCC 474).[236]

As a divine person he also possessed omniscient, divine knowledge. This means that Jesus' understanding of his divine identity was rooted in his divine person and so he could never have been like those hesitating Christs depicted in popular films. That doesn't mean, however, that Jesus had unlimited knowledge about everything.

Because Jesus truly became man, he had a human soul that possessed human knowledge. The *Catechism* says, "This knowledge could not in itself be unlimited: it was exercised in the historical conditions of his existence in space and time. This is why the Son of God could, when he became man, 'increase in wisdom and in stature, and in favor with God and man' [Luke 2:52]" (CCC 472).

As an analogy, you could read all the books about swimming ever written and still drown if you jumped into a lake. Knowing about how to swim is different from having the human knowledge of how to swim rooted in experience that helps develop proper reflexes and muscle memory. This means that Jesus probably learned human concepts and skills through instruction and practice like everyone else. Being God, he could have given himself these abilities through his attribute of omnipotence, but that was not necessary for his saving mission.

Admittedly, the Incarnation is a mystery and so we can't exhaust it with a simple model of how the all-knowing God could truly become a man and not a human-looking puppet. Pope Benedict XVI wrote, "It becomes quite apparent that he is true man and true God, as the Church's faith expresses it. The interplay between the two is something that we cannot ultimately define."[237] But even if we can't know everything about what the Incarnation allowed in Christ's human nature, there is one thing we know it did not allow: sin.

Pope St. John Paul II said, "We repeat with the New Testament, with the Creed, and with Vatican Council II that Jesus Christ 'has truly been made one of us, like us in all things except sin.' It is precisely thanks to this likeness that 'Christ, the final Adam, by the revelation of the mystery of the Father and his love, fully reveals man to man himself and makes his supreme calling clear'" (GS 22).[238]

Sacred Scripture, Sacred Tradition, and the teaching of the Magisterium are unanimous that Jesus Christ was, and still is, sinless. But not only did Jesus not sin, it was *impossible* for Jesus to sin because he is the God-man. God is perfect goodness itself, so a "sinful God" would be as logically contradictory as a square circle. And since Jesus is God, it follows that the act of sinning would be impossible for Jesus.

Some people think that Jesus could have sinned but (thankfully for us) he did not, but just because we can conceive of something in the mind does not mean it could really happen. Atheists often say they can "imagine" a universe without God even though God is a necessary being and so it is impossible for him to not exist. There can be no physical universe that exists without God also existing, regardless of what any of us can imagine.

But if Jesus could not have sinned, why did Satan even bother to tempt him (Matt. 4:1–11)? Satan isn't omniscient like God is, so he has to acquire knowledge, but his mind operates in a completely contrary way to the perfection that is found in God's wisdom. That means demons and the devil, as St. Thomas Aquinas says, "can be misled with regard to supernatural matters; for example, on seeing a dead man, they may suppose that he will not rise again, or, on beholding Christ, they may judge him not to be God."[239]

Ironically, some people promote the "flawed and failed" Jesus as a means to help people believe in him. They say there is nothing awe-inspiring in a Savior who could not have possibly failed, while others go further and say Jesus couldn't really be human if he never sinned.

Sin, however, is not an essential part of the human condition. Do those same critics think that an infant who dies shortly after baptism wasn't really human because he was without sin? Maybe they mean that being human (especially an adult with a conscience) involves struggling against temptations. But Jesus was not a holy robot, incapable of sinning because of perfect programming. He had—and has—a fully human nature, which means, as Hebrews 4:15 says, "We have not a high priest who is unable to sympathize with our weaknesses, but one who in every respect has been tempted as we are, yet without sin."[240]

Even though we are sinful human beings, we don't sin or even struggle with sin at every moment of our lives. When we temporarily lose ourselves in holy, joyful moments of life we see a glimpse of our restored human nature and the true happiness God wants for us. We don't need a "sinful savior" because he's allegedly more "approachable." We can't approach God in our originally sinful states in order to possess that glorified human nature. We are instead grateful that God "approached us" or that he came down to our level as a man in order to rescue us from sin, make us "truly human" and give us everlasting life.

We shouldn't stand in awe of Jesus because he avoided sinning in the way that a tightrope walker avoids plunging to his death. Instead, we should stand in awe of Jesus because he is God: the infinite act of being who, for our sake, humbled himself and became man. I trust in him for my salvation not because he is "really good" at being holy, but because holiness is a part of his nature and goodness ultimately comes from his divinity.

To say "Jesus I trust in you" does not mean we trust a person who managed not to fail or sin. It means we place our trust and hope for salvation in the most trustworthy reality imaginable, the all-powerful, all-knowing God who created us.

COUNTERFEITS
from
Protestants

16

Prosperity Preacher

I was sitting on the couch with my arms crossed while the credits rolled, when one of my friends asked me, "What did you think of the movie?"

"Aside from the subpar acting?" I replied. "I think it had a terrible message."

"What do you mean? It's a movie about people becoming Christian. What's so terrible about that?"

"Nothing," I said. "But the movie's message was that if you accept Jesus as your savior, your car will start running again, your wife won't be infertile anymore, and the football team you coach will win the big game. But the Christian life doesn't always work out that way. This movie preached a false prosperity gospel."

Prosperity theology, also called the *prosperity gospel* or the *health-and-wealth gospel*, can be traced back to the New Thought movement of late nineteenth-century America. Adherents of this movement, many of whom were not Christian, claimed that the mind had power over reality—power that could be used to cure disease or end poverty.[241]

Prosperity preachers took this mindset and applied it to Jesus' promises that whatever we give will be "given back to us" (Luke 6:38) and that if we ask anything in his name he will give it to us (John 14:14). So, if we just ask Jesus for health and wealth he will give it to us! According to a 2006 *Time* magazine survey, one-third of Christians believe, "If you give your money to God, God will bless you with more money."[242] They believe in a Jesus who wants us to have unending happiness not just in the life to come but in the life we have right now—and the only thing keeping us from this happiness is the refusal to ask for it.

But, how can that be true if . . .
. . . Jesus Promised Spiritual Rather Than Material Blessings

Prosperity theology became popular in the mid-twentieth century among Pentecostals who believed that a person could know that God favored him through the reception of spiritual gifts (or *charisms*). These gifts were usually things like prophecy or speaking in tongues, but the gifts of *prosperity* and *comfort* became a siren song among televangelists like Kenneth Copeland and Oral Roberts. They promised that God will bless people who plant "seed-faith"—give financial gifts—with even more money than they had given. This would happen because of what televangelist Robert Tilton called the "law of compensation." According to Roberts, "Luke 6:38 says, 'Give, and it will be given to you.' We must first plant a seed of faith so that God can multiply it back to meet our need."[243]

Copeland wrote in *Laws of Prosperity*, "Do you want a hundredfold return on your money? Give and let God multiply it back to you. No bank in the world offers this kind of return! Praise the Lord!"[244] Lest you think Copeland is being metaphorical, his wife Gloria describes the precise return believers can expect from their "investment":

You give $1 for the gospel's sake, and $100 belongs to you. Give $10 and receive $1,000. Give $1,000 and receive $100,000 . . . Give one airplane and receive one hundred times the value of the airplane. Give one car and the return would furnish you a lifetime of cars. In short, Mark 10:30 is a very good deal."[245]

Mark 10:30 and Luke 6:38 are favorite verses among prosperity preachers, but they don't contain unconditional promises of prosperity. Luke 6:38 is part of Jesus' Sermon on the Plain and teaches about being generous with mercy and forgiveness. At the end of the verse, Jesus says, "The measure you give will be the measure you get back." This parallels what Jesus said in the Sermon on the Mount: "With the judgment you pronounce you will be judged, and the measure you give will be the measure you get" (Matt. 7:2).

In Mark, Jesus promises, "There is no one who has left house or brothers or sisters or mother or father or children or lands, for my sake and for the gospel, who will not receive a hundredfold now in this time, houses and brothers and sisters and mothers and children and lands" (10:29–30). Now, if we aren't literally going to have hundreds of new family members in this life as a reward for leaving some, why should we believe that we'll literally have hundreds of new possessions? This verse is not about Jesus' guaranteed rate of return on your tithe but about God's care for those who have sacrificed their lives to serve him.

Other prosperity teachers cite Jesus' promise that "your Father who is in heaven give[s] good things to those who ask him" (Matt. 7:11). Leroy Thompson uses the analogy of a multimillionaire who has so much money that he doesn't bat an eye at buying his adult children a home with cash. He then asks, "How much more is God willing to do for his children? Do you believe God is *at least* a multimillionaire?"[246]

But here, too, Jesus is talking primarily about God giving us spiritual gifts, not material blessings. This is evident in the parallel passage in Luke 11:13, where Jesus says, "If you then, who are evil, know how to give good gifts to your children, how much more will the heavenly Father give the Holy Spirit to those who ask him!"

Thompson's own analogy also undermines his argument. Some wealthy people might buy their children whatever they want, but others raise their children to be self-reliant, to help them develop good character.[247] If God is *at least* as wise as these wealthy men, then maybe he will not automatically give us wealth because he wants something for us that money cannot provide.

Finally, some cite John 14:14, where Jesus promises, "If you ask anything in my name, I will do it." One prosperity preacher says, "When we pray, believing that we have already received what we are praying, God has no choice but to make our prayers come to pass."[248]

But prayer is not magic; God is not a genie in a lamp. He will grant only what we ask in accordance with his will. That this is the meaning of John 14:14 is made clear by the evangelist in his first epistle, where he says, "And this is the confidence which we have in him, that if we ask anything *according to his will* he hears us" (1 John 5:14).

. . . Wealth Can Lead to Damnation

Some people quote the Bible as saying, "Money is the root of all evil," but what the Bible actually says is, "The love of money is the root of all evil" (1 Tim. 6:10). It's not a sin to be wealthy, and the Bible records several wealthy people, such as Abraham and Job, who found favor with God. But although money is not sinful in itself, it can easily become an *opportunity* for sin. Far from saying that believers would be blessed with money, therefore, Jesus warned that "it is easier for a camel to go through the eye of a needle than for a rich man to enter the kingdom of God" (Matt. 19:24).

Some people downplay these words by claiming that the "eye of the needle" was actually a small gate in the old city of Jerusalem that a camel could pass through only once it shed the belongings it carried on its sides. By this we're meant to understand that Jesus was teaching that a rich person must shed his excess belongings if he wants to enter the kingdom of heaven. But according to New Testament scholar David Croteau, this interpretation is farfetched:

> There is no mention of a gate in any of the passages. Matthew 19:24, Mark 10:25, and Luke 18:25 neglect to reference a gate. None of them says Jesus was pointing to a gate in Jerusalem. In fact, Mark 10:32 says they started on the road toward Jerusalem. Jesus was not even in Jerusalem when referring to the supposed "needle gate." The whole concept of a gate is entirely imported into the text.[249]

It's more likely that Jesus was talking about an actual sewing needle and an actual camel, using hyperbole to caution how wealth can be a hindrance to salvation—not a reward for faithfulness.

When prosperity preachers claim that God blesses the faithful with money, they resurrect the attitudes of Jews in Jesus' time who believed that wealth signified a person's favor (or lack of favor) with God. But Jesus corrected that idea, noting that God "sends rain on the just and on the unjust" (Matt. 5:45) and that the eighteen men who died when the tower of Siloam fell on them were not worse than the other inhabitants of Jerusalem (Luke 13:4).

Who will be blessed with wealth or called to endure poverty? That is not decided simply by the use of a special prayer or commitment to tithe. Rather, it is decided by the sovereign will of God that providentially orders our freely chosen acts according to his divine plan. God may let foolishness cause someone to be poor, but he might also allow someone to become poor through no fault of his own because of an illness, economic downturns, or a natural disaster.

Being impoverished does not mean a person failed to follow God's will. God has a special concern for the poor (Psalm 34:6), and believers have a special obligation to help the poor (Luke 14:14, 1 John 3:17). James says, "Has not God chosen those who are poor in the world to be rich in faith and heirs of the kingdom which he has promised to those who love him?" (2:5).

. . . Jesus Wasn't Rich

The ultimate argument against prosperity preachers is impoverished Christians. Why don't sincere believers have "plenty of money" or "their best life now?" Rather than face the obvious truth that God doesn't always bless us with material prosperity even if we strive to do his will, prosperity teachers end up blaming the individual for his poverty.

Prosperity preachers make excuses like "They didn't follow God's will" or "They weren't being generous enough" to explain why God hasn't blessed them. Setting aside the ludicrous idea that the difference between poor Christians and rich Christians is that the latter more closely follow God's will, there is an easy counterexample to this argument: the real Jesus Christ.

Since he was God incarnate, we know that Jesus was without sin (Heb. 4:15) and he *always* did the Father's will (John 5:19). Wouldn't the Father have rewarded Jesus' faithfulness with abundant wealth? In the ancient world, there was no comfortable middle class, just relative poverty and luxurious wealth. Jesus was not destitute or a beggar, but he was also not wealthy. The Bible says Jesus became poor (2 Cor. 8:9), taking the form of a slave (Phil. 2:7) and had nowhere to rest his head (Luke 9:58).

The fact that Jesus was not among the wealthy during his earthly ministry strikes a deathblow to the promises of prosperity preachers, so some of them try to make biblical arguments that Jesus was actually rich. For example, Thomas Anderson, the senior pastor of the Living Word Bible Church in Mesa, Arizona, tries to make that case by pointing out that the Roman soldiers cast lots for Jesus' tunic and that he had a moneybag for his disciples to watch.[250]

Any set of clothes, however, would have been valuable in the ancient world, so it makes sense the soldiers would have wanted Jesus' garments. Also, any sum of money the disciples kept in a bag would pale in comparison to the amount stored in a treasure room that would have made someone rich. Besides, if Jesus were rich he would have been given a dignified execution and not have been crucified among the lower classes.

Jesus' constant admonishments of "the rich" make it even more implausible that he belonged to that social class. As David Fiensy observes, "In the eyes of the elite, Jesus would still have been poor. Compared to their luxurious lifestyle, he must have lived very simply and humbly. The socioeconomic distance between Jesus and the elite classes—even if he did come from a comfortable family—was enormous."[251]

Ironically, prosperity preachers fail to emphasize the real riches Jesus came to give those who believe in him. They are like children who are obsessed with the presents their parents buy them at Christmas and only pay lip service to the love and affection those material gifts represent. St. Paul tells us, "You know the grace of our Lord Jesus Christ, that though he was rich, yet for your sake he became poor, so that by his poverty you might become rich" (2 Cor. 8:9).

Jesus did not become man so that we wouldn't have any problems in this life because we could buy whatever we want. Those aren't the "riches" of which Paul speaks. Instead, God became man so we could be rich in his *grace* and through it be able to persevere no matter what evils we encounter.

Jesus said, "In the world you have tribulation; but be of good cheer, I have overcome the world" (John 16:33). As our faith in God matures, he doesn't reward us by giving us everything we want, he helps us *want everything he gives*: both comfortable and uncomfortable. Paul put it well: "I have learned, in whatever state I am, to be content. I know how to be abased, and I know how to abound; in any and all circumstances I have learned the secret of facing plenty and hunger, abundance and want. I can do all things in [Christ] who strengthens me" (Phil. 4:11–13).

A Sacrifice Only for Some

In January of 2017, I debated Protestant apologist James White on the question, "Can a Christian lose his salvation?" The majority of the Protestants in attendance were Calvinists whose theology emphasizes God's sovereignty over everything that happens. So, when my opening slide presentation failed to display on screen I got a laugh by saying, "I guess for most of you here that was foreordained, so what can you do?"[252]

Throughout the debate, White argued that God does not cooperate with man in order to secure a person's salvation (a view he condemns as "synergism"). Instead, God alone chooses who will be saved and he gives only these people "irresistible" saving grace that they cannot reject. These saved people (or the "elect") do not accept God's offer of salvation; God's grace simply saves them no matter what. This irresistible grace ensures that they will never reject his offer of salvation, either at the first moment they are saved or at any moment after that.

But this view leads to consequences that even many Protestants reject.

The Calvinist scholar A.W. Pink said of Jesus' death on the cross, "Not one for whom he died can possibly miss heaven."[253] This means that if Jesus died for a believer it is impossible for that person to ever lose his salvation (a belief Calvinists call the "perseverance" or "preservation" of the saints). It also means, according to some Calvinists, that Jesus did *not* die on the cross for people who will "miss heaven" and be damned. This means Jesus did not die for all of humanity; or as a friend of mine once quipped, "Here's an idea for a bumper sticker, 'Jesus might have died for you!'"

But how can that be true if . . .
. . . God Wants All People to Be Saved

St. Paul urged that "supplications, prayers, intercessions, and thanksgivings be made for all men" (1 Tim. 2:1). He considered this good in his sight because God "desires all men to be saved and to come to the knowledge of the truth" (1 Tim. 2:4). The only obstacle to a person spending eternal life with God is the person's own refusal to repent from his sin and accept the grace Christ merited for him on the cross.

This saving grace is available to all people, but it won't have the same *effect* in every person. Those who accept God's offer of salvation and remain in his friendship will have made God's grace *efficacious*. Their free choices allowed the effects of God's grace to become manifested in their lives and prepare them to enter into the joy of heaven after death.

Even for those who have yet to believe or have fallen away from the Faith, God's grace is waiting for them in sacraments like baptism or reconciliation. These create or restore friendship with God and so their saving effects are present to everyone in at least a potential way. That is why Paul said that God "is the Savior of all men, especially of those who believe" (1 Tim. 4:10). God makes salvation available to all even if all do not choose to receive it.

Calvinists usually reply by saying that God desires the salvation of all "kinds" of men even if he doesn't desire that every one of them go to heaven. For example, in 1 Timothy 2:1 Paul says, "First of all, then, I urge that supplications, prayers, intercessions, and thanksgivings be made for all men, for kings and all who are in high positions, that we may lead a quiet and peaceable life, godly and respectful in every way."

If God did desire all people to be saved, they would all be saved, since salvation is 100 percent up to God. But since Scripture talks about people not being saved (Matt. 7:14, 25:46), the only logical explanation is that God actually does not want those people to be saved. So, in verses like 1 Timothy 2:1, Calvinists say that Paul is talking about praying for all *kinds* of men, both rich and poor, rather than for every single human being.[254] This is pleasing to God because God desires people from every social status to be saved, even if he does not desire that every person be saved.

But desiring the salvation of all people and desiring the salvation of all kinds of people are not mutually exclusive. We could imagine a crew member on the Titanic rebuking a fellow crew member who refused to help save poorer third-class passengers by saying, "Our job is to help all passengers, including third class and everyone in low positions, because we have to save all passengers." Just as the crew member will not let prejudice about social classes keep him from saving all the souls onboard, God desires peace in human relationships so that all people can have the opportunity to hear the gospel and be saved.

Even if Paul were emphasizing that we should pray for people in all social classes rather than for all people in general, this doesn't detract from his wish for *all people* to live in peace, which pleases a God who wants all people to be saved. The atheistic scholar Richard Carrier, who has no vested interest in either side of this theological debate, says that Paul "is telling people to pray for peace, on behalf of everyone alive, but in [verse four] he is describing what God wants . . . there is simply no other way to interpret what Paul is saying except that what God actually wants is all people, not *some of all kinds of people*, to be saved and to come to a knowledge of the truth."[255]

And, because God wants all people to be saved, he has made the salvation of anyone a real possibility; this means that Christ indeed offered his life as a sacrifice for every human being. St. John affirmed that Christ "is the expiation for our sins, and not for ours only but also for the sins of the whole world" (1 John 2:2).

. . . Jesus Died for All Men

Christ made salvation possible for all people, but that salvation only becomes actual for those who choose to receive it through baptism (1 Pet. 3:21, John 3:5) and through persevering in faith (Matt. 10:22). Calvinists usually say in response that 1 John 2:2 is talking about how Christ died not just for the saved in his local community of Christians but for all saved people throughout the entire world. However, this interpretation is farfetched because when John talks about the "world" he means the *entire* world, including unbelievers.

For example, 1 John 5:19 says, "We know that we are of God, and the whole world [*ho kosmos holos*] is in the power of the evil one." This verse does not mean that *only* believers are under the power of the devil but that all people throughout the entire world suffer from the devil's temptations. Yet, these same words are found in 1 John 2:2, which says Christ atones not just for our sins "but also for the sins of the whole world [*ho kosmos holos*]." Southern Baptist David Nelson states:

> In John 1 and 12 *kosmos* is used in the sense of both the earth and all the inhabitants of the earth, indicating that in the incarnation Jesus came to earth for the sake of saving all who would believe in him . . . to say that world refers to 'all the elect' or 'all without distinction' (i.e. all kinds, classes, or ethnicities) strains the plain meaning of the text.[256]

There are verses in the Bible that describe Jesus dying for certain groups of people and even for individuals. Paul declared to the Galatians, "I live by faith in the Son of God, who loved me and gave himself for me" (2:20). Of course, just because Jesus died for Paul it doesn't follow that Jesus died *only* for him. Similarly, when the Bible says Jesus died for his "friends" (John 15:13) or his "sheep" (John 10:11), it doesn't mean Jesus atoned only for the sins of those who would come to believe in him. What the Calvinist needs to show is a Bible verse that says Jesus *only* died for the elect, and this he cannot do.

But what about when Jesus said, "The Son of Man came not to be served but to serve, and to give his life as a ransom for many" (Matt. 20:28)? If he truly died for all people, shouldn't it say that Jesus gave his life as "a ransom for all"?

It should be noted that Paul does say Christ "gave himself as a ransom for all" (1 Tim. 2:6), but there is also no contradiction in describing a person as saving "many people" and "all people" in the same situation.

When Captain "Sully" Sullenberger landed a crippled jet on the Hudson River in 2009, his actions saved all 155 passengers and crew on board. But a person could have also said to Sully after the rescue, "Wow, captain, you saved many lives today." Likewise, Jesus' death on the cross atoned for the sins of the whole world and made salvation possible for the many people who inhabit it. Jesus died for all people and "many" ended up being ransomed, allowing the effects of his death to be applied to their souls.

. . . Jesus Warned About the Loss of Salvation

John 3:16 is sometimes called "the football verse" because Christians often hold it up on signs at football games hoping it will be seen when television cameras pan across the crowd. In this verse, John tells us, "For God so loved the world that he gave his only Son, that whoever believes in him should not perish but have eternal life." Some Protestants take this to mean that a person who believes in Jesus will definitely be saved in the future and so he can't possibly lose his salvation. But that is not what Jesus taught.

In John 15, Jesus called himself "the true vine" and said that we are the branches because our spiritual life flows from him into each one of us. He then declared:

> "I am the vine, you are the branches. He who abides in me, and I in him, he it is that bears much fruit, for apart from me you can do nothing. If a man does not abide in me, he is cast forth as a branch and withers; and the branches are gathered, thrown into the fire and burned" (John 15:5–6).

In the parable of the unforgiving servant, Jesus describes a king forgiving a servant's debt and how that servant then refused to forgive a much smaller debt that a fellow servant owed him. The king was outraged at hearing this and said, "You wicked servant! I forgave you all that debt because you besought me; and should not you have had mercy on your fellow servant, as I had mercy on you?'" (Matt. 18:33) The king then threw the servant in jail and demanded he repay the debt the king previously forgave.

After relating this parable, Jesus told the crowd, "So also my heavenly Father will do to every one of you, if you do not forgive your brother from your heart" (Matt. 18:35). Notice that the king in this parable represents God, so Jesus is saying that God can forgive our "debts" (an ancient Jewish metaphor for sins) but then revoke that forgiveness if we continue to gravely sin. According to the Protestant New Testament scholar Mel Shoemaker, "A failure to forgive others may result in the forfeiture and loss of the Father's forgiveness and our salvation."[257]

In response to these verses, some Calvinists cite Jesus' teaching in John 6 as proof that a believer's salvation cannot be lost. In this part of the Bread of Life discourse, Jesus says, "All that the Father gives me will come to me; and him who comes to me I will not cast out" (John 6:37). Indeed, Jesus will not cast out a believer that God's grace has moved to have faith in him. But, that doesn't mean the person can't later reject Jesus and cast *himself* out of Christ's presence. Paul describes this scenario when he writes, "By rejecting conscience, certain persons have made shipwreck of their faith" (1 Tim. 1:19).

Jesus then says, "This is the will of him who sent me, that I should lose nothing of all that he has given me, but raise it up at the Last Day" (John 6:39). St. John Chrysostom tells us that Jesus means, "At least *for my part*, I will not lose them." So in another place, declaring the matter more clearly, he said, 'I will not reject anyone who comes to me.'"[258]

In the next verse, Jesus adds, "For this is the will of my Father, that everyone who sees the Son and believes in him should have eternal life; and I will raise him up at the Last Day." But once again, notice the use of present tense verbs: it is not those who "saw" the Son at one time or "believed" in him at another who will be saved. It is those who *continue* to see and believe in him until death. White even admitted in his own book on the subject that "the present tense refers to a continuous, on-going action.... The wonderful promises that are provided by Christ are not for those who do not truly and continuously believe."[259]

Jesus did not teach that a single act of belief in the past or present guarantees a person's admittance into heaven. A person must continually believe in Jesus and choose to remain in communion with him until death in order to have eternal life. That's why Jesus said it is not the one who believes that will be saved but that "he who endures to the end will be saved" (Matt. 10:22). John himself said just a few verses after John 3:16 that "he who believes in the Son has eternal life; he who does not *obey* [emphasis added] the Son shall not see life, but the wrath of God rests upon him" (3:36).

The Anti-Catholic with No Face

My family and I were strolling through San Diego's Balboa Park when I came across a street preacher with a cart full of evangelism tracts. I glanced through a few of them before the man approached me saying, "See any you like? They're free!"

"I'm familiar with these tracts. I'm Catholic" I replied.

"Oh!" he said with an excited tone. "Then you'll want to see *these*."

He then handed me tracts with titles like *Are Catholics Christian?* and *Why Is Mary Crying?* Their author was Jack Chick, an enigmatic cartoonist who passed away a few years ago but whose legacy lives on in the millions of tracts that bear his name. Although their topics differ, they almost always end with a deceased person coming face-to-face with a terrifying, fifty-foot tall, faceless Jesus sitting on a throne condemning him to everlasting torment.

Jesus is faceless in these tracts because Chick, like other Fundamentalists, believed that creating images of people in heaven violates Exodus 20:4–5's command against creating "graven images." Even though these verses condemn idolatry (not artistry), Chick took no chances. That's why his Jesus is just a robed, white silhouette, which adds to the surreal, almost macabre visual style of his tracts.

In one on Catholicism, a man pleads with this colossal Christ, "But I went to Mass! I was a good person!" In response, the emotionless "judge Jesus" thunders back at the man about the need to trust in him alone and not "traditions of men" like the Catholic Mass. If the man had done this, he would have known that engaging in the sin of idolatry (which includes worshipping Christ in the Eucharist) is a surefire way to hear Jesus tell him on Judgment Day, "Depart from me you accursed, into the everlasting fire!"

It's appropriate that our last counterfeit Christ is actually a polar opposite of the first one we examined: the non-judgmental buddy. This counterfeit is a terrifying judge who has no reservations about damning anyone who does not accept him as "personal Lord and Savior."

But how can that be true if . . .

. . . Jesus Never Said He Is Our "Personal Lord and Savior"

At the end of another tract, called *This Is Your Life*, Chick describes a person who makes "the right choice" when it comes to salvation. This man says, "Of course I believe the Bible—and I'm convinced that I am lost and going to hell—but what must I do to be saved?" The answer comes from a preacher who emphatically declares, "Repent! Surrender your life to Christ, acknowledge that he died for your sins and receive him as your savior!" The man then prays a variant of what has come to be known as the Sinner's Prayer: "Lord, I know I'm a sinner. I repent of my sins and I acknowledge Jesus Christ as my Lord and personal Savior!"

Considering how important this prayer is in Evangelical Christianity, you would think it came right from Scripture. But instead it dates to the 1940s. Even Protestant apologists like Matt Slick admit, "There is not a single verse or passage in Scripture, whether in a narrative account or in prescriptive or descriptive texts, regarding the use of a 'Sinner's Prayer' in evangelism. *Not one.*"[260]

Some Protestants claim that the episode involving "the good thief on the cross" proves that, though perhaps the *formula* behind the Sinner's Prayer is not found in the Bible, its *essence* is. The thief says to Jesus, "Remember me when you come in your kingly power," to which Jesus replies, "Truly, I say to you, today you will be with me in paradise" (Luke 23: 42–43). They say that the thief's confession of faith and request to Jesus saves him, proving the worth of the Sinner's Prayer.

But God's saving people through such extraordinary means does not nullify the *ordinary* means he gave for our salvation. For example, many Protestants believe that infants who die before they have faith in Christ can still go to heaven, but that wouldn't prove that adults who are able to make an act of faith don't have to in order to be saved.

And, contrary to what many Protestants believe, the Bible tells us that salvation is a *process* rather than a single act like saying the Sinner's Prayer. This is evident in the multiple answers Jesus gave when it came to the subject of what we must do to be saved:

- "Truly, truly, I say to you, unless one is born of water and the Spirit, he cannot enter the kingdom of God" (John 3:5).

- "If you would enter life, keep the commandments" (Matt. 19:17).
- "This is the work of God, that you believe in him whom he has sent" (John 6:29).
- "He who eats my flesh and drinks my blood has eternal life, and I will raise him up at the Last Day" (John 6:54).

Jesus believed salvation consisted of receiving baptism, having faith, persevering in good works, and obeying the Ten Commandments. That's why the *Catechism* says, "All men may attain salvation through faith, baptism and the observance of the commandments" (2068). But part of observing the commandments includes honoring the Lord's Day and receiving Jesus in the Eucharist, about which Jesus said, "Unless you eat the flesh of the Son of Man and drink his blood, you have no life in you" (John 6:53).

. . . Jesus Commanded Us to Celebrate the Eucharist

In one tract, ominously named *The Death Cookie*, Chick claims that the Eucharist is derived from pagan idolatry and the devil gave this idol to the founders of the Catholic Church so they could control the masses.[261] One of the biggest whoppers in this tract (and there are so many to choose from) is the claim that the letters *IHS* on the eucharistic host refer to the Egyptian gods Isis, Horus, and Seb. (In reality, they are the first three letters in the Greek transliteration of Jesus' name, which is spelled IHSOYS and is pronounced "Iesous.")

After this fanciful history lesson, the comic portrays a hooded figure telling frightened believers, "If you don't obey us we won't let you eat the Jesus cookie anymore. And that means you'd *lose* your immortal souls." This same priest warns the pope, "If the people ever read what's in the sacred writings . . . then they will find out we've tricked them."

But in spite of the Catholics' efforts to hide the Bible, the people find it and discover they've been tricked: because Jesus said of the Eucharist, "Do this in remembrance of me" (Luke 22:19). "Then it's symbolic," the humble believer declares, "The Holy Papa [the pope] has *lied* to us."

If Jesus' words were "purely symbolic," why didn't Jesus correct those who misunderstood him? After his Bread of Life discourse in John chapter 6, those who heard him, including his disciples, said, "How can this man give us his flesh to eat?" (John 6:52) and, "This is a hard saying; who can listen to it?" (John 6:60). John then tells us that, "After this many of his disciples drew back and no longer went about with him" (John 6:66).

Yet on another occasion, when Jesus' disciples mistakenly thought he was talking about literal food, he did correct them. In that case, Jesus explained the symbolic meaning: "My food is to do the will of him who sent me, and to accomplish his work" (John 4:34). However, instead of doing this again after giving the Bread of Life discourse, Jesus reaffirmed his literal meaning, and the Twelve continued to follow him. They did so because they knew Jesus had, as Peter said, "the words of eternal life" (John 6:68).

Moreover, the words "in remembrance" or "in memory" from Luke 22:19 come from the Greek word *anamnesis*, which involves more than a mere mental recollection of a past event or person. It has the significance of a "remembrance brought about by the act of sacrifice." The Lutheran scholar Joachim Jeremias informs us:

The command to repeat the rite is not a summons to the disciples to preserve the memory of Jesus . . . it is an eschatologically oriented instruction: "Keep joining yourselves together as the redeemed community by the table rite, that in this way God may be daily implored to bring about the consummation on the [Second Coming]."[262]

A biblical example of this kind of *memorial sacrifice* can be found in Leviticus 24:7–8, where the Israelite priest and his sons are instructed to offer a memorial sacrifice of bread to the Lord each Sabbath. The verses say, "And you shall put pure frankincense with each row, that it may go with the bread as a memorial portion to be offered by fire to the LORD. Every sabbath day Aaron shall set it in order before the LORD continually on behalf of the people of Israel as a covenant forever." The original Hebrew word for "memorial" in this passage, *azkarah*, also means "memorial offering." The parallel between this and the sacrifice of the Mass, at which holy bread is offered on the new Sabbath to commemorate the new, everlasting covenant in Christ, is uncanny.

So when Jesus said, "Do this in memory of me," he did not mean simply, "Remember me when you eat this meal." A more accurate translation of Jesus' command would be, "Receive me as a memorial sacrifice." The first Christians, who were raised in Judaism, would have had no difficulty understanding that a memorial dinner can bring about the actual presence of God.[263] Bible scholar Brant Pitre puts it this way:

Just as God had been really present to his people in the tabernacle of Moses and the temple of Solomon, so now Jesus would be really and truly present to his disciples through the Eucharist. And just as the old bread of the Presence had been the sign of God's "everlasting covenant," so now the Eucharist would become the perpetual sign of the new covenant, sealed in his blood.[264]

. . . Jesus Established One Church

After I flipped through this street preacher's tracts, I tried to find some common ground. "I get what you're trying to do," I said, "but Chick tracts aren't a great way to go about it. I mean he endorses some pretty wild conspiracy theories."

"Like what?"

"Well, like the idea that the Vatican has a secret archive of every Protestant in the United States and that the Jesuits are working behind the scenes to take over the world."

He smiled, and without skipping a beat replied, "Well, your new pope is a Jesuit. Is he not?"

Seeing that the conversation was going nowhere fast, I decided to keep my promise to my children that they would get to see the train museum and not (pardon the pun) derail it with an impromptu Catholic-Protestant debate. So I wished this preacher well before giving him my contact information. But before I left I grabbed a few more of his tracts to research more of the false claims they made about Christ.

One such claim, also commonly found in other Protestant literature on Church history, is that Jesus never established a single Church for all believers. Instead, Jesus established our *salvation;* "the Church" he founded is just the invisible bond that exists between everyone who receives that salvation. These critics claim that a single, visible, hierarchical, and universal Church did not come into existence until Emperor Constantine made Christianity the official religion of the Roman Empire in the fourth century. Pastor John MacArthur even said that this event "launches a thousand years of the dark ages. Where religion and relationship to God is not personal. The Church is a surrogate for God. You connect to the Church. You don't connect by faith."[265]

But this is wrong for a number of reasons.

First, Emperor Constantine did not make Christianity the official religion of the Roman Empire: Emperor Theodosius did that in the year 381 (Constantine just granted Christians legal toleration, about seventy years before). Also, the term "dark ages" is politically loaded and imprecise. MacArthur doesn't even use it in its common academic sense— to refer to the centuries following the fall of Rome and the barbarian invasions. He imagines that period extending over a millennium to include most of pre-Reformation Christendom. Yet Christians traditionally believed that the time *before* the fifth century was "dark" because the world was shrouded in pagan darkness. For the next ten centuries, the light of Christ spread all over the world because of the dreaded "institutions" the Catholic Church provided to it.

Second, prior to this time the Church was not a loose collection of believers who simply "believed in Jesus." Instead, Christians recognized a sacred order, or hierarchy, and they encountered God through the Church he gave us. St. Cyprian of Carthage wrote in the early third century, "You *cannot have* God for your Father if you do not *have* the *Church* for your *mother*."[266] St. Ignatius of Antioch exhorted believers at the beginning of the second century, "Follow the bishop even as Jesus Christ does the Father."[267]

A single authoritative Church is also found in the New Testament, such as where Jesus said that, in the case of a fellow Christian who sins against you, as a last resort you should "tell it to the Church; and if he refuses to listen even to the Church, let him be to you as a Gentile and a tax collector" (Matt. 18:17). Jesus is not talking about a local congregation (or "your church") but *the* Church as one body of believers.[268] Jesus did not pray for there to be hundreds of differing denominations that would be united only by an ambiguous "belief in Jesus." Instead he prayed that believers "may become perfectly one, so that the world may know that you have sent me and have loved them even as you have loved me" (John 17:23).

And *contra* MacArthur and other critics like him, a personal relationship with Jesus, by itself, does not guarantee a Christian's salvation.

The Bible says that there are passages in it that are confusing, passages that people twist to their own destruction (2 Pet. 3:16). This destruction can come through a misreading of Scripture that creates a counterfeit Christ who teaches grave errors. These errors can be related, for example, to the nature of God (like denials of the Trinity), the nature of the good (like condoning homosexual behavior), or the nature of grace (like teaching that salvation can never be lost).

If someone has a personal relationship with the *real* Jesus, he would know that Jesus wants us to have more than conversations with him in prayer. He wants us to receive his grace in the sacraments, especially the Eucharist and reconciliation, and to have a sure foundation for our beliefs through the Church, the "pillar and foundation of truth" he established (1 Tim. 3:15, Matt. 16:18). Jesus warned that "false Christs and false prophets will arise" (Matt. 24:24) but through the wisdom of his bride, the Church (Eph. 5:32) we can be confident that Christ—the real Jesus Christ—is with us "always, to the close of the age" (Matt. 28:20).

WHO DO YOU SAY THAT I AM?

In the region of Caesarea Philippi in Israel there is a tranquil river that flows in the shadow of a large rock that juts out of the earth. A pious tradition holds that this was the spot where Jesus asked his disciples, "Who do men say that the Son of Man is?" (Matt. 16:13).

Given the natural temptation to gossip and spread the latest news, most of the disciples were quick to say what *other people* thought about Jesus. "Some say John the Baptist, others say Elijah, and others Jeremiah or one of the prophets," they responded. Maybe they were hoping to hear Jesus admonish those people's incorrect answers, or perhaps Jesus would reveal if someone had stumbled upon the right answer. But Jesus, as he was often prone to do, did not meet their expectations.

"But who do you say that I am?"

At first they were speechless. How humiliating would it have been to publicly admit you misunderstood your master's identity in the presence of your brother disciples? Perhaps it'd be better to say nothing than to be wrong, so they remained silent until one disciple spoke up. His name was Simon and he was marked by an impulsiveness that can be helpful or harmful, depending on the situation. He declared, "You are the Christ, the Son of the living God."

Jesus turned to him but didn't affirm his intellect or clever wit. He instead declared, "Flesh and blood has not revealed this to you, but my Father who is in heaven." Perhaps turning to the large rock behind all of them to use as a symbol of the solid foundation he would become, Jesus said to Simon, "You are Peter, [which means "rock" in Greek] and on this rock I will build my Church, and the powers of death shall not prevail against it."

Like Moses and David before him, Peter was chosen to lead God's people not because of his strengths but in spite of his weaknesses. Peter's faith was not something he cultivated through his own piety and hard work. Lest he get that idea, Jesus told him that it was not human ingenuity ("flesh and blood") but supernatural grace that moved Peter to get "the right answer" about Jesus's identity. St. Paul confirms that "no one can say 'Jesus is Lord' except by the Holy Spirit" (1 Cor. 12:3).

My goal in these pages has been to help people overcome the obstacles that might be holding them back from receiving this same gift of faith. It is my heartfelt prayer that they see that Jesus Christ was not a deceased prophet, preacher, zealot, or guru. He's not even a "was"—like every other deceased person in history. Rather, Jesus *is* the living and resurrected Son of God who came to earth to redeem and save mankind. He is fully God and fully man, the mediator between humanity and divinity and he wants you, personally, to know him.

So, how can people come to know Jesus and find in him salvation from their sins? First, they must *repent*. In Greek, the word is *metanoia,* which literally means "to be of another mind." One who repents changes the direction of his life and signals that he no longer wants to sin. A person who repents must then *believe* that Jesus Christ is God's Son who has come to redeem us from sin and give us grace to become adopted children of God. This grace doesn't just hide our sins or make us appear righteous: it actually transforms us so that we become holy, so that we become "partakers of the divine nature" (2 Pet. 1:4).

Finally, a person must *receive* the grace of God into his life. According to Jesus' instruction, this involves first being baptized, which washes away the stain of sin and incorporates us into the Body of Christ. Then, a Christian is able to participate in the sacraments of the Church, like the Eucharist, through which we receive even more grace— the unearned gift of God that allows us to have his divine life within us and makes us "new creations" in Christ (2 Cor. 5:17).

I'd like to close with one last piece of evidence for Jesus being more than a man, a piece of evidence that is more intuitive than logically deductive. You either see it or you don't.

When you say the names of Muhammad, Buddha, Confucious, or L. Ron Hubbard in polite company, you might be seen as knowledgeable, worldly, or esoteric. But when you say "Jesus Christ," there is a tension that immediately fills the air. There is just something different about that name, that person.

Some people may say that those who bristle at the name "Jesus Christ" do so at the intolerance and hatred that have been committed in his name. But the same visceral reaction doesn't accompany words like "Christian" or "Catholic." Instead, I contend that this name has power unlike any other name when it is uttered because it belongs to a person who has power unlike any other.

By saying this name we place ourselves, whether we realize it or not, under the glare of the eternal and almighty God become man. Paul said of Jesus, "God has highly exalted him and bestowed on him the name which is above every name, that at the name of Jesus every knee should bow, in heaven and on earth and under the earth, and every tongue confess that Jesus Christ is Lord, to the glory of God the Father" (Phil 2:9–11).

The questions that are left for us are, "Will we confess that Jesus is Lord in our hearts and let him be the true Lord of our lives" (even when we want that job)? and "Will we confess that Jesus is Lord to those who disagree, even stridently?"

I pray that, for all of us, the answer to both will be not just a "Yes," but a spirit-filled "Amen!"

COUNTERFEIT CHRISTS
IN POLITICS

Throughout this book we have met many counterfeit Christs. These made-up versions of Jesus clearly contradict who Jesus really is, what he taught, and how he lived.

Sometimes, though, people make claims about what Jesus would support but it's not easy to tell if there's a counterfeit involved. Especially in politics.

"What would Jesus do" about gun control, the minimum wage, immigration, or criminal justice reform? If Jesus casts a ballot, would it be for a Republican, a Democrat, or a third-party candidate? Would he support tax bill A, B, or C?

In these specific cases we don't have information from divine revelation or the teaching of the Church to give us the same kind of certainty and specificity we have when it comes to basic doctrinal and moral truths. For these questions we must use what is called "prudential judgment"—and this can lead to Christians reasonably disagreeing with one another. According to the *Catechism*:

> *Prudence* is the virtue that disposes practical reason to discern our true good in every circumstance and to choose the right means of achieving it . . . With the help of this virtue we apply moral principles to particular cases without error and overcome doubts about the good to achieve and the evil to avoid (CCC 1806).

Now, pointing out that sometimes political questions involve prudential judgments doesn't mean that *all* judgment is reserved to the individual, so Catholics can do whatever they want. Because prudence is concerned with choosing the *good*, a prudential judgment does not reflect a merely subjective preference. So we can be held morally accountable for the judgments we make in these matters.

Neither are questions involving prudential judgment like the question, "Which ice cream flavor should I eat?"—questions about matter of taste that have no right answer. But unlike principles of doctrine and morality, the Church has not definitively taught which specific answers the faithful should embrace when it comes to implementing moral principles—like justice or care for the poor—in the public sphere. And in some cases, differing geographical, cultural, social, or economic circumstances could change which answer is most appropriate for a given community.

That's why individual Catholics can propose their own answers to these questions—provided that those answers are faithful to the explicit teachings of the Church—without being guilty of presenting a counterfeit Christ.

For example, consider the question, "Should we raise the minimum wage?" Everyone can agree that it's a revealed and non-negotiable truth that Jesus wants us to help the poor. A solution like "social Darwinism" that proposes we ought to let the poor die out is simply off the table.

But the Church has not described in every detail *how* we should help the poor. It's a prudential matter, a matter of what is practically most effective, so believers can disagree on (and better still, constructively debate with solid evidence) whether something like a minimum-wage increase accomplishes that goal.

Catholics are free to disagree with one another on these matters without being guilty of endorsing sin, *even if their disagreement is with a bishop or the pope.* The Congregation for the Doctrine of the Faith taught, "When it comes to the question of interventions in the prudential order, it could happen that some magisterial documents might not be free from all deficiencies. Bishops and their advisors have not always taken into immediate consideration every aspect or the entire complexity of a question."[269]

This does not mean that the prudential judgments of the Magisterium carry no weight when we make our own judgments and so they can just be ignored. The CDF also said, "It would be contrary to the truth, if, proceeding from some particular cases, one were to conclude that the Church's Magisterium can be habitually mistaken in its prudential judgments, or that it does not enjoy divine assistance in the integral exercise of its mission."[270]

What the Church teaches on matters involving prudential judgment, either through the teachings of the pope in an encyclical or the recommendations of the colleges of bishops, should be given proper consideration. For example, the United States Conference of Catholic Bishops says in its *Faithful Citizenship* voting guide:

> Prudential judgment is also needed in applying moral principles to specific policy choices in areas such as armed conflict, housing, health care, immigration, and others. This does not mean that all choices are equally valid, or that our guidance and that of other Church leaders is just another political opinion or policy preference among many others. Rather, we urge Catholics to listen carefully to the Church's teachers when we apply Catholic social teaching to specific proposals and situations. The judgments and recommendations that we make as bishops on such specific issues do not carry the same moral authority as statements of universal moral teachings. Nevertheless,

the Church's guidance on these matters is an essential resource for Catholics as they determine whether their own moral judgments are consistent with the Gospel and with Catholic teaching.[271]

So where can a counterfeit Christ show up in these conversations? He doesn't arrive when someone merely proposes that one political position instead of another is more consistent with (or effective in promoting) the teachings of Jesus. Instead, a counterfeit Christ emerges when someone declares that Jesus would support a particular prudential judgment with the same certainty we have on revealed matters of doctrine and morals—and so good Christians *must* support this judgment or else be guilty of disobeying the teachings of Christ.

For example, in 2012, Speaker of the House Paul Ryan proposed a federal budget that some critics claimed stood in contradiction to Ryan's own Catholic values. Headlines included accusations like, "Jesus would oppose the Paul Ryan budget" and "Paul Ryan's budget not what Jesus would do." The *National Catholic Reporter's* John Allen Jr. asked Archbishop Chaput, "What about the wing of the Church that says a party that supports the Ryan budget also ought to cause concern?" The archbishop may have had the more radical charges against the Ryan budget in his mind when he replied:

Jesus tells us very clearly that if we don't help the poor, we're going to go to hell. Period. There's just no doubt about it. That has to be a foundational concern of Catholics and of all Christians. But Jesus didn't say the government has to take care of them, or that we have to pay taxes to take care of them. Those are prudential judgments.

Anybody who would condemn someone because of their position on taxes is making a leap that I can't make as a Catholic. . . . You can't say that somebody's not Christian because they want to limit taxation. Again, I'm speaking only for myself, but I think that's a legitimate position. It may not be the correct one, but it's certainly a legitimate Catholic position; and to say that it's somehow intrinsically evil like abortion doesn't make any sense at all.[272]

The counterfeits can be especially egregious when those who claim to definitively know Jesus' position on matters involving prudential judgment arrive at their conclusions through bad exegesis of Scripture.

Returning to the question of what specific tax rates Jesus would support, Erika Christakis writes in *Time* magazine, "As near as we can tell, Jesus would advocate a tax rate somewhere between fifty percent (in the vein of "If you have two coats, give one to the man who has none") and 100 percent (if you want to get into heaven, be poor). Mostly, he suggested giving all your money up for the benefit of others."[273]

David Barton, representing the other end of the spectrum, believes Jesus would barely tax people at all. He describes capital gains taxes as "a tax on profits" and says that this is anti-biblical because in Scripture, "the more profit you make the more you are rewarded. Both the parable of the talents (Matt. 25:14-30) and the parable of the minas [talents] (Luke 19:12-27) conflict with the notion of a tax on capital gains."[274]

What *did* Jesus say about taxes? Well, when he was asked, he simply said, "Render to Caesar what is Caesar's, and to God what is God's" (Matt. 22:21). His teaching that we should give our personal possessions to those in need is not a revelation of (contrary to what Christakis asserts) the precise rate at which government should tax income. When it comes to Barton's claim, Jesus did *not* say, "The more profit you make, the more you are rewarded." The parable of the talents refers to our responsibility to respond to God's grace and use it to help others instead of ignoring these spiritual gifts.

What could make Barton's and Christakis' descriptions of Jesus into counterfeits is not the knowledge what Jesus actually believed the opposite of what they ascribe to him. Fact is, we just don't know with moral certainty what Jesus would say about cutting capital gains taxes or imposing a marginal tax rate of fifty percent or more. People can, of course, make arguments that the teachings of Jesus line up better with one prudential judgment over another or that one specific policy carries out Jesus' teaching more effectively than another.

But these things are different from the assertion that a certain prudential judgment points to the *only* position a Christian can hold—or the only party a Christian can belong to, or the only candidate or ballot measure a Christian can vote for—because that's what Jesus wants.

To assert this is to manufacture yet another counterfeit Christ, employing the Savior as an ideological weapon rather than docilely listening to what he has revealed about himself.

ENDNOTES

Introduction

1   Pope Benedict XVI, *Jesus of Nazareth* (New York: Doubleday, 2007), xv–xvi.

2   "The Hitchens Transcript" December 17, 2009. Available online at:
     https://www.pdxmonthly.com/articles/2009/12/17/christopher-hitchens.

Chapter 1
Non-Judgmental Buddy

3   Robert A.J. Gagnon, *The Bible and Homosexual Practice: Texts and Hermeneutics*
     (Nashville, TN: Abingdon Press, 2001), 212.

4   Dan Barker, *Godless: How an Evangelical Preacher Became One of America's Leading
     Atheists* (Berkeley, CA: Ulysses Press, 2008), 181–183.

5   C.S. Lewis, *Mere Christianity* (New York: Harper One, 1980), 53.

6   In chapter ten we will address how Jehovah's Witnesses mistranslate this verse in
     order to avoid its obvious meaning.

7   Robert M. Bowman Jr. and J. Ed Komoszewski, *Putting Jesus in His Place: The Case for
     the Deity of Christ* (Grand Rapids: Kregel Publications, 2007), 97.

8   For a response to claims of this kind against this specific verse see Douglas McCready,
     He Came Down from Heaven: The Preexistence of Christ and the Christian Faith
     (Wheaton, IL: InterVarsity Press, 2005), 149–150.

9   William Lane Craig, *Reasonable Faith* 3rd ed. (Wheaton, IL: Crossway Books, 2008),
     310–312.

10   For a rebuttal of the claim that Jesus really was a liar or a lunatic see Karlo Broussard,
     Prepare the Way (El Cajon, CA: Catholic Answers Press, 2018), 141–148.

11   Neely Tucker, "The Book of Bart" *The Washington Post*, March 5, 2006. Available
     online at: http://www.washingtonpost.com/wp-dyn/content/article/2006/03/04/
     AR2006030401369.html.

Chapter 2
Victim of Conspiracies

12   Dan Brown, *The Da Vinci Code* (New York: Random House, 2003), 307.

13   "When the bishop of Oea (modern Tripoli) introduced Jerome's recent rendering
     into his community service, Augustine worriedly related, the congregation nearly
     rioted. (At issue, perhaps, was the identity of the vine under which the prophet Jonah
     had rested—a 'gourd' so the traditional version, or an 'ivy' so Jerome; Letter 75.7, 22;
     Jonah 4:6)." Paula Fredriksen, *Augustine and the Jews: A Christian Defense of Jews and
     Judaism* (New Haven, CT: Yale University Press, 2010), 289."

14   Charles Freeman, *A New History of Early Christianity* (New Haven, CT: Yale
     University Press, 2009), 215.

15   Bruce M. Metzger and Bart D. Ehrman, *The Text of the New Testament: Its Transmission,
     Corruption, and Restoration* (New York and Oxford: Oxford University Press, 2005), 126.

16   David Alan Black, *New Testament Textual Criticism: A Concise Guide* (Grand Rapids, MI: Baker Academic, 1994), 18.

17   *The Text of the Earliest New Testament Greek Manuscripts*, eds. Philip Wesley Comfort, David P. Barrett (Wheaton, IL: Tyndale House Publishers, 2001), 17.

18   "Of the Greek literature created before 250 B.C. we have only a small, even though very valuable, part. We do not even have the complete works of those authors who were included in the lists of classics compiled by the Alexandrian philologists. Of all the works of pagan Greek literature perhaps only one percent has come down to us." Rudolf Blum, *Kallimachos: The Alexandrian Library and the Origins of Bibliography*, trans. Hans H. Wellisch (Madison, WI: University of Wisconsin Press, 1991), 8.

19   F.F. Bruce, *The Books and the Parchments* (Revell, NJ: Old Tappan, 1963), 78.

20   Dan Brown, *The Da Vinci Code* (New York: Random House, 2003), 307.

21   *Letter to the Smyrneaans*, 2.

22   "The Gospel of Philip cannot claim a first-century date. It belongs to the same second- and third-century period as most of the Gnostic Nag Hammadi texts." Andrew Phillip Smith, *The Gospel of Philip* (Woodstock, VT: Skylight Paths Publishing, 2005), xiii.

23   Ariel Sabar, "Karen King Responds to 'The Unbelievable Tale of Jesus's Wife'" *The Atlantic*, June 16, 2016. Available online at: https://www.theatlantic.com/politics/archive/2016/06/karen-king-responds-to-the-unbelievable-tale-of-jesus-wife/487484/.

24   Craig Blomberg, *The Historical Reliability of the Gospels* (Downer's Grove, IL: IVP Academic, 2007), 264.

25   *Letter to the Ephesians*, 18.

26   *Apology of Aristedes*, 2.

27   As Peter T. O'Brien says in his commentary on Colossians: "*Theotes* ('deity') is the abstract noun from *theos* ('God') and is to be distinguished from *eiotes* ('divine nature,' 'quality'), the abstract from *theios* ("divine," Rom. 1:20; Wis. 18:19; cf. Lightfoot, 179, who illustrates the difference between the two nouns in Plutarch's *Moralia*). The former is *deitas*, the being God, i.e. the divine essence or Godhead; the latter is *divinitas*, i.e. the divine quality, godlikeness (Meyer, 358). Meyer adds: 'Accordingly, the *essence* of God, undivided and in its whole fullness, dwells in Christ in his exalted state, so that He is the essential and adequate image of God (i. 15), which he could not be if he were not possessor of the divine 'essence.'" *Word Biblical Commentary: Vol. 44: Colossians, Philemon, 110*. See also W.E. Vine. *Vines Complete Expository Dictionary of Old and New Testament Words: With Topical Index* (Nashville, TN: Thomas Nelson, 1996), 178–179.

28   "The most natural way to read Titus 2:13, then, in light of its own literary style and theology, is to see 'Jesus Christ' as in apposition to 'our great God and savior.'" Daniel B. Wallace, *Granville Sharp's Canon and Its Kin: Semantics and Significance* (New York: Peter Lang Publishing, 2009) 263.

29   Dan Brown, *The Da Vinci Code* (New York: Random House, 2003), 306.

30   Bart D. Ehrman, *Truth and Fiction in The Da Vinci Code* (New York: Oxford University Press, 2004), 15.

31   "Two bishops, Theonas and Secundus, refused to sign and were sent into exile—a momentous event, as it marked the first time in Church history that a secular punishment (exile) was applied to an ecclesiastical crime (heresy)." Steve Weidenkopf, *Timeless: A History of the Catholic Church* (Huntington, IN: Our Sunday Visitor, 2018), 59.

Chapter 3
Man of Mystery

32   C.S. Lewis, "Christian Apologetics" in *God in the Dock* (Grand Rapids: Wm. B. Eerdmans, 1970), 93.

33   D.M. Murdock, *Who Was Jesus?: Fingerprints of the Christ* (Seattle, WA: Stellar House Publishing, 2011), 256.

34   Joel B. Green, "The Gospel According to Mark" in *Cambridge Companion to the Gospels*, ed. Stephen C. Barton, (Edinburgh: Cambridge University Press, 2006), 141.

35   A few 19th-century scholars argued that Tacitus' works were forgeries composed by other authors but their "extreme hypothesis," in the words of Van Voorst, never gained a following. Robert Van Voorst, *Jesus Outside the New Testament: An Introduction to the Ancient Evidence* (Grand Rapids: Wm. B. Eerdmans, 2000), 42. See also Clarence W. Mendell, *Tacitus: The Man And His Work* (New Haven, CT: Yale University Press, 1957), 219.

36   Specifically it is cited in Commentary on Zechariah 3:14. Andreas Mehl, *Roman Historiography*, trans. Hans-Friedrich Mueller (West Sussex, UK: Wiley Blackwell, 2011), 146.

37   St. Augustine writes, "How can we be sure of the authorship of any book, if we doubt the apostolic origin of those books which are attributed to the apostles by the Church which the apostles themselves founded[?] . . . any one who denies their authorship is answered only by ridicule, simply because there is a succession of testimonies to the books from the time of Hippocrates to the present day, which makes it unreasonable either now or hereafter to have any doubt on the subject. How do we know the authorship of the works of Plato, Aristotle, Cicero, Varro, and other similar writers, but by the unbroken chain of evidence? So also with the numerous commentaries on the ecclesiastical books, which have no canonical authority, and yet show a desire of usefulness and a spirit of inquiry." (Augustine, *Contra Faustum*, Book XXXIII).

38   Eusebius, *Church History* 3:39.

39   Brant Pitre, *The Case for Jesus: The Biblical and Historical Evidence for Christ* (New York: Image, 2016), 22.

40   Based on testimony from the early Church Fathers, Pope Benedict XVI endorsed the view that another John, known in Scripture as John the Presbyter, was a major influence behind the fourth Gospel. He writes, "At any rate, there seem to be grounds for ascribing to 'Presbyter John' an essential role in the definitive shaping of the Gospel [of John], though he must always have regarded himself as the trustee of the tradition he had received from the son of Zebedee." Pope Benedict XVI, *Jesus of Nazareth*, (New York: Doubleday, 2007), 226.

41   I've heard this claim articulated in personal conversation and also found Murdock asserting, "When scientifically scrutinized, the historical record clearly demonstrates the emergence of the gospels at the end of the second century." D.M. Murdock, *Who Was Jesus?: Fingerprints of the Christ* (Seattle, WA: Stellar House Publishing, 2011), 256.

42   The earliest complete biography of Buddha is Asvaghosa's *Buddhacarita* was written 500 years after the Buddha's death, while one of the earliest complete sources for Alexander is Diodorus Siculus's *Bibliotheca historica*, which was written about 300 years after his death.

43   "[E]ven two generations are too short a span to allow the mythical tendency to prevail over the hard historic core of the oral tradition." A.N. Sherwin-White, *Roman Society and Roman Law in the New Testament* (Oxford: Clarendon Press, 1963), 190.

44   Ibid., 187.

45 "[T]hey have at least as much in common with Graeco-Roman *Bioi*, as the *Bioi* have with each other. Therefore, the gospels must belong to the genre of *Bios*." Richard A. Burridge, *What Are the Gospels?: A Comparison with Graeco-Roman Biography* (Grand Rapids: Wm. B. Eerdmans, 2004), 250.

46 Bart Ehrman, *Jesus, Interrupted: Revealing the Hidden Contradictions in the Bible (and Why We Don't Know About Them)* (New York: HarperOne, 2009), 48.

47 Specifically, Cassius Dio says Nero set the fire and watched it from the roof of his palace (*Roman History* 62.16–17), Suetonius says Nero set the fire and watched from the tower of Maecenas (*The Life of Nero*, 12), and Tacitus says it is uncertain who started the fire and that Nero was 30 miles away in Antium when it happened (*Annals*, 15.38–39).

48 Michael Grant, *Jesus: An Historian's Review of the Gospels* (New York: Charles Scribner's Sons, 1977), 176.

49 The classic work on this topic is J.J. Blunt's *Undesigned Coincidences in the Writing of both the Old and New Testaments* (1869). A modern treatment can be found in Lydia McGrew, *Hidden in Plain View: Undesigned Coincidences in the Gospels and Acts* (Chillicothe, OH: DeWard, 2017).

50 E.P. Sanders, *Judaism: Practice and Belief, 63 BCE-66 CE* (Minneapolis, MN: Fortress Press, 2016), 212.

51 See for example Richard Bauckham, *Jesus and the Eyewitnesses: The Gospels as Eyewitness Testimony* (Grand Rapids: Wm. B. Eerdmans, 2017).

52 Peter J. Kreeft and Ronald K. Tacelli, *Handbook of Catholic Apologetics* (San Francisco: Ignatius Press, 2009), 171.

Chapter 4
Mythical Messiah

53 The debate can be viewed online here: https://www.youtube.com/watch?v=RQA DiuyPV80&t=4057s.

54 Bart Ehrman, *Did Jesus Exist? The Historical Argument for Jesus of Nazareth* (New York: HarperOne, 2012), 4.

55 Timothy Freke and Peter Gandy, *The Jesus Mysteries: Was the "Original Jesus" a Pagan God?* (New York: Three Rivers Press, 1999), 134.

56 John Meier, *A Marginal Jew: Rethinking the Historical Jesus*, Vol. I (New York: Doubleday, 1991), 56.

57 F.F. Bruce, *Jesus and Christian Origins* (Grand Rapids: Eerdmans, 1974), 23. Pilate is mentioned in the works of Jewish writers like Philo and Josephus, but this portion of Tacitus's writings is the only ancient pagan document that mentions him.

58 Bart Ehrman, "Fuller Reply to Richard Carrier," April 25, 2012. Available online at: https://ehrmanblog.org/fuller-reply-to-richard-carrier/.

59 James D.G. Dunn, *Jesus Remembered: Christianity in the Making* (Grand Rapids: Wm. B. Eerdmans, 2003), 141.

60 Robert Van Voorst, *Jesus Outside the New Testament: An Introduction to the Ancient Evidence* (Grand Rapids: Wm. B. Eerdmans, 2000), 83. For a response to Carrier's argument that this is an interpolation see Tim O'Neill, "Richard Carrier is Displeased Again" October 17, 2018. Available online at: https://historyforatheists.com/2018/10/richard-carrier-is-displeased-again/.

61 C.H. Dodd, *The Apostolic Preaching and Its Developments*, 2nd edition (London: Hodder and Stoughton, 1944), 16.

62   Other explanations for how James could be a non-literal brother of a "spiritual Jesus"
      fare no better. For example, Earl Doherty claims "brother of the Lord" is a figurative
      title and that James, "seems to have been the head of a community in Jerusalem
      which bore witness to the spiritual Christ . . . My own [explanation] would be that
      the Jerusalem sect known to Paul began a number of years earlier as a monastic group
      calling itself 'brothers of the Lord.'" Earl Doherty, *Jesus: Neither God nor Man* (Ottawa:
      Age of Reason Publications, 2009), 61. However, Doherty offers no evidence for the
      existence of such a group in first-century Jerusalem. It's simply proposed as a way to
      resolve the massive problem Jesus' relative poses for the mythicist hypothesis. In a
      similar vein, Robert Price claims the title of "brother" may have been given to James
      because he was committed to Jesus' ideals in a way that surpassed any of the other
      disciples, including Peter. Price points to a nineteenth-century messiah in China
      who called himself "Jesus' little brother" as proof of his theory that "brother" could
      simply mean spiritual follower. Robert Price, *The Christ Myth Theory and its Problems*
      (Cranford, NJ: American Atheist Press, 2011), 352. But now we're really grasping at
      straws if Christians who lived thousands of years and miles away from Jesus are the
      only way to explain the habits of first-century believers.
63   Bart Ehrman, *Did Jesus Exist? The Historical Argument for Jesus of Nazareth* (New York:
      HarperOne, 2012), 146.
64   Richard Carrier, *On the Historicity of Jesus* (Sheffield: Sheffield Phoenix Press, 2014),
      446–447.
65   Bart Ehrman, *Did Jesus Exist? The Historical Argument for Jesus of Nazareth* (New York:
      HarperOne, 2012), 14–15.

Chapter 5
Pagan Copycat

66   Joseph Atwill, *Caesar's Messiah: The Roman Conspiracy to Invent Jesus* (Charleston, SC:
      CreateSpace, 2011) 39.
67   "One hates to be so severe in the analysis of the work of an innovative thinker who
      gives us the gift of a fresh reading of familiar texts, but in the present case it is hard
      to euphemize. The reading given here is just ludicrous." Available online at: http://
      www.robertmprice.mindvendor.com/rev_atwill.htm.
68   "The literary sources here are few but unmistakable: Mithra was known as the rock-
      born god." Manfred Clauss. *The Roman Cult of Mithras: The God and His Mysteries*,
      trans. Richard Gordon (New York: Routledge, 2001), 62.
69   "There was no death of Mithras." R.L. Gordon, "Mithraism and Roman Society:
      Social factors in the explanation of religious change in the Roman Empire,"
      Religion, Vol. 2, Issue 2, Autumn 1972, pg. 96. Edwin Yamauchi says, "I know of no
      references to a supposed death and resurrection." Quoted in Lee Strobel, *The Case for
      the Real Jesus* (Grand Rapids: Zondervan, 2007), 172.
70   Tom Harpur, *The Pagan Christ* (New York: Walker and Company, 2004), 5.
71   W. Ward Gasque, "The Leading Religion Writer in Canada ... Does He Know
      What He's Talking About?" *History News Network*. Available online at: https://
      historynewsnetwork.org/article/6641.
72   "Isis conceived Horus after Osiris's death by means of Osiris's reanimated male
      member." Susan A. Stephens, *Seeing Double: Intercultural Poetics in Ptolemaic Alexandria*
      (Los Angeles: University of California Press, 2003), 56.

73   Stanley E. Porter and Stephen J. Bedard, *Unmasking the Pagan Christ: An Evangelical Response to the Cosmic Christ Idea* (Toronto: Clements, 2006), 67.

74   "Set then cuts his brother's body into fourteen pieces and scatters them about the delta; the body is later reconstructed by Isis and her son Horus, who collect the fragments in a boat made of acacia wood, although they never find the phallus. Osiris, resurrected, then goes on to reign as God of the Dead in the underworld." Ben A. Heller *Assimilation/generation/resurrection* (London, Bucknell University Press, 1997), 52.

75   Carsten Claussen, "Turning Water to Wine: Re-reading the Miracle at the Wedding in Cana" in *Jesus Research: An International Perspective* eds. J.H. Charlesworth and Petr Pokorny (Grand Rapids: Wm. B. Eerdmans, 2009), 85–86.

76   Giulia Sfameni Gasparro, *Soteriology and Mystic Aspects in the Cult of Cybele and Attis* (Leiden: E.J. Brill, 1985), 48.

77   Kersey Graves, *The World's Sixteen Crucified Saviors* (Boston: Colby and Rich Publishers, 1876), 113.

78   See https://infidels.org/library/historical/kersey_graves/16/.

79   *First Apology*, 66.

80   "Mithraism, that is a cult of Mithras claiming Persian origin and described as a `Mystery', was the last such cult to appear in the West, in the middle of the second century A.D., long after the appearance of Christianity." R.L. Gordon, "Mithraism and Roman Society: Social factors in the explanation of religious change in the Roman Empire," *Religion*, Vol. 2, Issue 2, Autumn 1972, pg. 93. There was a Persian god named Mithra (also called Mitra) whose name was found in a treaty that is dated to 1400 B.C. However, this Persian god (who was invoked to uphold contracts) was not the same warrior deity worshipped among Roman soldiers who is alleged to be the model for Jesus.

81   J.P. Kane, "The Mithraic Cult Meal" in *Mithraic Studies: Proceedings of the First International Congress*, Vol. 2, ed. John R. Hinnells (Manchester: Manchester University Press, 1975), 316.

82   Bart D. Ehrman, *How Jesus Became God: The Exaltation of a Jewish Preacher from Galilee* (New York: HarperOne, 2015) 11–13.

83   Although, in his study of ancient biographies Tomas Hägg claims Philostratus invented the story of this commission, it doesn't make his alleged biography any more reliable. He writes, "If we suppose that Damis was invented by Philostratus as an authentic looking contemporary source and an effectual foil to Apollonius, it follows that Julia Domna's 'commission' of him is fabricated as well." Tomas Hägg, *The Art of Biography in Antiquity* (Cambridge: Cambride University Press, 2012), 325.

84   Maria Dzielska, *Apollonius of Tyana in Legend and History*, trans. Piotr Pienkowski (Rome: L'erma di Bretschneider, 1986), 187.

85   *On the Embassy to Gaius*, 38.

86   T.N.D. Mettinger. *Riddle of Resurrection: "Dying and Rising Gods" in the Ancient Near East*, Coniectanea Biblica, Old Testament, 50 (Coronet Books, 2001), 221.

87   Ibid., 18.

88   Gerd Ludemann, What Really Happened to Jesus? (Louisville: Westminster, John Knox Press, 1995), 80.

Chapter 6
Rotting Corpse

89   The debate can be viewed online at: https://www.youtube.com/watch?v=bIuDfh-6iUs.

90 Dan Barker, *Godless: How an Evangelical Preacher Became One of America's Leading Atheists* (Berkeley, CA: Ulysses Press, 2008), 294–295.

91 John Ziesler, *Pauline Christianity* (New York: Oxford University Press, 1990), 98.

92 *City of God*, 13.20.

93 Dan Barker, *Godless: How an Evangelical Preacher Became One of America's Leading Atheists* (Berkeley, CA: Ulysses Press, 2008), 295.

94 Ibid.

95 Dan Barker, *Godless: How an Evangelical Preacher Became One of America's Leading Atheists* (Berkeley, CA: Ulysses Press, 2008), 302.

96 Trent Horn, *Why We're Catholic: Our Reasons for Faith, Hope, and Love* (El Cajon, CA: Catholic Answers Press, 2017), 55–56.

97 *Contra Celsum*, 2.55.

98 Carolyn Osiek, "The women at the tomb: What are they doing there?" *HTS Teologiese Studies / Theological Studies* 53 (1997), 109.

99 Both men are referenced in Josephus (*Antiquities* 20.8.6, 20.5) and the Acts of the Apostles (21:38, 5:36).

100 N.T. Wright, "Christian Origins and the Resurrection of Jesus: The Resurrection of Jesus as a Historical Problem" July 12, 2016. Available online at: http://ntwrightpage. com/2016/07/12/christian-origins-and-the-resurrection-of-jesus-the-resurrection-of-jesus-as-a-historical-problem/.

Chapter 7
Rabbi Yeshua

101 See, for example, Stan Telchin's story of his conversion from Judaism in his 1981 book simply titled, *Betrayed!*.

102 Robert Van Voorst, *Jesus Outside the New Testament: An Introduction to the Ancient Evidence* (Grand Rapids: Wm. B. Eerdmans, 2000), 117–119.

103 Shmuley Boteach, *Kosher Jesus* (Gefen Publishing House, Jerusalem, 2012), 150.

104 Cited in Michael L. Brown, *Answering Jewish Objections to Jesus: General and Historical Objections* (Grand Rapids, MI: Baker Books, 2003), 158.

105 Other people claim that the New Testament is anti-semitic because it unjustly makes the Jewish people responsible for Jesus' death. However, that some Jewish leaders and citizens of Jerusalem were involved in Jesus' death is a historical fact. As we saw in chapter three, Josephus said Pilate executed Jesus "because of an accusation made by the leading men among us." Maimonides, one of the greatest Jewish thinkers in history, said, "Jesus of Nazareth… held the opinion that he would be the Messiah but was killed in the courthouse [the Jewish leadership in the Sanhedrin]." Cited in Richard G. Marks, *The Image of Bar Kokhba in Traditional Jewish Literature: False Messiah and National Hero* (University Park, PA: Pennsylvania State University Press, 1994), 91. Just because some first-century Jews were directly involved in the death of Jesus doesn't mean all Jewish people share in their guilt. The truth is that *everyone*— Jews and Gentiles, you and I—are responsible for the death of Jesus because it was our sins that Christ bore on the cross. The Second Vatican Council taught, "The Jewish authorities and those who followed their lead pressed for the death of Christ; still, what happened in his passion cannot be charged against all the Jews, without distinction, then alive, nor against the Jews of today. Although the Church is the new people of God, the Jews should not be presented as rejected or accursed by God, as if this followed from the holy scriptures." *Nostra Aetate*, 4.

106 In one case, a non-Jewish king named Cyrus the Great (who was instrumental in bringing the Jewish people out of exile) was called a messiah (Isa. 45:1).

107 *First Apology*, 50.

108 Gerald Sigal, *Isaiah 53: Who is the Servant?* (Xlibris, 2007), Kindle edition.

109 Another prophecy related to the crucifixion that is often overlooked is found in Matthew 27:43, where the priests mock Jesus on the cross by saying, "He trusts in God; let God deliver him now, if he desires him; for he said, 'I am the Son of God.'" Some people say this is a reference to Psalm 22:8 ("let him rescue him, for he delights in him!"), but that verse does not mention "the Son of God." However, the deuterocanonical book of Wisdom says, "For if the righteous man is God's son, he will help him, and will deliver him from the hand of his adversaries" (2:18). Most modern Jews reject the inspiration of deuterocanonical books like Wisdom, but that was not true of Jews who lived before and shortly after the time of Christ. Fragments of the deuterocanonical books have been found among the Dead Sea Scrolls and they were penned in a special style that was unique to books that were considered inspired Scripture. For more on the inspiration of these books see Trent Horn, *The Case for Catholicism: Answers to Classic and Contemporary Protestant Objections* (San Francisco: Ignatius Press, 2017), 54–74.

110 Michael L. Brown, *Answering Jewish Objections to Jesus: Messianic Prophecy Objections* (Grand Rapids, MI: Baker Books, 2003), 50.

111 N.T. Wright, "Jerusalem in the New Testament" Originally published in *Jerusalem Past and Present in the Purposes of God*. Ed. P. W. L. Walker (Grand Rapids, MI: Baker, 1994), 53–77. Available online at: http://ntwrightpage.com/files/2016/05/Wright_Jerusalem_New_Testament.pdf.

112 Pinchas Lapide, *The Resurrection of Jesus: A Jewish Perspective* trans. Wilhelm C. Linss (Eugene, OR: Wipf and Stock, 2002), 126.

113 The Testament of Simeon, 7. Available online at: http://www.newadvent.org/fathers/0801.htm.

114 "Progress must have seemed terribly slow during the first century—the projected total is only 7,530 by 100." Rodney Stark, *The Rise of Christianity* (New York: HarperCollins, 1997), 7–8. For the Jewish population see "Populousness of the Jews" in *Jewish Life and Thought Among Greeks and Romans: Primary Readings*, eds. Louis H. Feldman and Meyer Reinhold (Minneapolis, MN: Fortess Press, 1996), 192. For the global population in the first century see Toshiko Kaneda and Carl Haub, "How Many People Have Ever Lived on Earth," Population Refrence Bureau, March 9, 2018, Available online at: https://www.prb.org/howmanypeoplehaveeverlivedonearth/.

115 "The plan of salvation also includes those who acknowledge the Creator, in the first place amongst whom are the Muslims; these profess to hold the faith of Abraham, and together with us they adore the one, merciful God, mankind's judge on the last day" (CCC 841). Note that Muslims "profess to hold the faith of Abraham," not that they possess the actual faith of Abraham because Islam, in what it teaches in the Quran, goes beyond what is revealed in the Bible and contradicts it.

116 Pinchas Lapide, *The Resurrection of Jesus: A Jewish Perspective*, trans. Wilhelm C. Linss (Eugene, OR: Wipf and Stock, 2002), 142–143.

117 Jacob Neusner, *A Rabbi Talks with Jesus* (Montreal: McGill-Queen's University Press, 2000), 32, 85.

118 Pope Benedict XVI, *Jesus of Nazareth: From the Baptism in the Jordan to the Transfiguration*, trans. Adrian J. Walker (New York: Doubleday, 2007), 110.

Chapter 8
Prophet Named Isa

119 Tzvi Lev, "Muhammad most popular baby name in Israel," *Arutz Sheva*, September 17, 2017. Available online at: http://www.israelnationalnews.com/News/News.aspx/235620.

120 Quranic translations taken from https://quran.com/.

121 Nabeel Qureshi, "The convert: Why I left Islam to follow Jesus," *Premier*. Available online at: https://www.premier.org.uk/Topics/Church/Apologetics/The-convert-Why-I-left-Islam-to-follow-Jesus.

122 Robert Van Voorst, *Jesus Outside the New Testament: An Introduction to the Ancient Evidence* (Grand Rapids: Wm. B. Eerdmans, 2000), 17.

123 Meraj Ahmad Meraj, "Literary Miracle of the Quran," International Journal of Humanities & Social Science Studies Vol. 3, No. 3 (November 2016), 320.

124 Ali Dashti, *Twenty Three Years: A Study of the Prophetic Career of Mohammad* (Costa Mesa: Mazda, 1994), 48–49.

125 John Dominic Crossan, *Jesus: A Revolutionary Biography* (San Francisco: HarperCollins, 2009), 163.

126 The fourteenth-century apocryphal Gospel of Barnabas claims that it was Judas Iscariot getting his comeuppance by being crucified in Jesus' place.

127 "The words used here do not negative that Jesus was nailed to the cross; they negative his having expired on the cross as a result of being nailed to it. That Jesus died a natural death is plainly stated in [sura] 5:117. The Gospels contain clear testimony showing that Jesus Christ escaped death on the cross." Maulana Muhammad Ali, *English Translation of the Holy Quran* (Wembley, U.K.: Ahmadiyya Anjuman Lahore Publications, 2010), 133.

128 See for example "Crucifixion or Cruci-Fiction" by Ahmed Deedat (available online at: http://uwkeuze.net/wp-content/uploads/2014/11/Crucifixion-or-Crucifiction-Ahmed-Deedat.pdf) or Shabir Ally vs. William Lane Craig, "Hoax or History? Did Jesus Rise from the Dead?" (2009). Available online at: https://www.reasonablefaith.org/media/debates/hoax-or-history-did-jesus-rise-from-the-dead1/.

129 Scholar Gabriel Said Reynolds argues that the Quran only says *the Jews* did not kill or crucify Jesus. They *thought* they did, but it was really God who ordained that Jesus would be crucified, only using the Jewish authorities to accomplish his will. This idea is even reflected in Acts 2:23, which says Jesus was "delivered up according to the definite plan and foreknowledge of God" to be "crucified and killed by the hands of lawless men." Reynolds admits that this view of the crucifixion is a kind of litmus test for Muslim orthodoxy and that almost all Muslims hold that Jesus did not die on the cross. Gabriel Said Reynolds, "The Muslim Jesus: Dead or Alive?" *Bulletin of SOAS*, Vol. 72, No. 2 (2009), 237. This kind of exegesis, though, can be helpful in introducing open-minded Muslims to the reasonableness of the Christian faith by showing where it "echoes" the Quran. This doesn't mean that we should contradict Christian doctrine; only that we should remove as many unnecessary obstacles as possible to someone coming to believe in Jesus Christ as our God and Savior. See also Ali Ibn Hassan, "Islam and the Crucifixion," *Catholic Answers Magazine Online*, October 23, 2017. Available online at: https://www.catholic.com/magazine/online-edition/islam-and-the-crucifixion-0.

130 See Trent Horn, *Hard Sayings: A Catholic Approach to Answering Bible Difficulties* (San Diego: Catholic Answers Press, 2016), 335–345.

131 See http://www.answering-christianity.com/john20_28.htm.

132 "John 20:28, no matter which variant or manuscript one chooses, is categorically secure for referring to Jesus as *theos*." Brian J. Wright, "Jesus as Theos: A Textual Examination" in *Revisiting the Corruption of the New Testament: Manuscript, Patristic, and Apocryphal Evidence* (Grand Rapids: Kregel, 2011), 250.

133 Bart D. Ehrman, *How Jesus Became God: The Exaltation of a Jewish Preacher from Galilee* (New York: HarperOne, 2015), 4.

Chapter 9
New Age Guru

134 See http://wisdomofchopra.com/.

135 Deepak Chopra, "The Illusion of Past, Present, Future," *The Huffington Post*, March 18, 2010. https://www.huffingtonpost.com/deepak-chopra/the-illusion-of-past-pres_b_326250.html.

136 Conversely, problems with our consciousness can also make diseases like cancer worse, or as Chopra says, "To say that a patient's awareness is responsible for his cancer is very troublesome to many people – and so it should be." Deepak Chopra, *Quantum Healing: Exploring the Frontiers of Mind/Body* Medicine (New York: Bantam, 2015), 308.

137 Deepak Chopra, *The Third Jesus: The Christ We Cannot Ignore* (New York: Three Rivers Press, 2008), 4.

138 Ibid., 10.

139 Bart Ehrman informs us, "Today there is not a single recognized scholar on the planet who has any doubts about the matter. The entire story was invented by Notovitch, who earned a good deal of money and a substantial amount of notoriety for his hoax." Bart Ehrman, *Forged: Writing in the Name of God* (New York: HarperCollins, 2011), 254.

140 Robert Van Voorst, *Jesus Outside the New Testament: An Introduction to the Ancient Evidence* (Grand Rapids: Wm. B. Eerdmans, 2000), 17.

141 David Van Biema. "Deepak Chopra on Jesus," *Time* magazine, November 13, 2008. Available online at: http://content.time.com/time/arts/article/0,8599,1858571,00.html.

142 Bart Ehrman, *Jesus, Apocalyptic Prophet of the New Millennium* (New York: Oxford University Press, 1999), 78.

143 Marcus Borg, *Jesus and Buddha: The Parallel Sayings* (Berkeley, CA: Ulysses Press, 1997), xiii.

144 Dhammapada 10:1, Leviticus 19:34.

145 Marcus Borg, *Jesus and Buddha: The Parallel Sayings* (Berkeley, CA: Ulysses Press, 1997), xiv.

146 "Seeing the danger of such miracles, I dislike, reject and despise them." Sutta 11.5 of the *Digha Nikaya*.

147 Sister Vajirā and Francis Story. *Last Days of the Buddha: The Mahāparinibbāna Sutta* (Sri Lanka: The Buddhist Publication Society, 2000), 29.

148 Deepak Chopra, *The Third Jesus: The Christ We Cannot Ignore* (New York: Three Rivers Press, 2008), 140.

149 Ibid.

150 Robert M. Price, *Top Secret: The Truth Behind Today's Pop Mysticisms* (Amherst, NY: Prometheus Books, 2008), 72.

151 Ibid.

152 David Van Biema, "Deepak Chopra on Jesus" *Time* magazine, November 13, 2008. http://content.time.com/time/arts/article/0,8599,1858571,00.html

153 W. Leonard, "The Gospel of Jesus Christ according to St John," *A Catholic Commentary on Holy Scripture*, eds. B. Orchard, E.F. Sutcliffe, R.C. Fuller, and R. Russell (New York: Thomas Nelson and Sons, 1953), 1001.

154 Cited in Ilaria Ramelli, "Luke 17:21: 'The Kingdom of God is Inside You' The Ancient Syriac Versions in Support of the Correct Translation," *Hugoye: Journal of Syriac Studies*, Vol. 12, No. 2 (2009), 279.

155 Deepak Chopra, *The Third Jesus: The Christ We Cannot Ignore* (New York: Three Rivers Press, 2008), 212.

Chapter 10
Jehovah's Greatest Creation

156 For more about this religious organization I recommend my booklet *20 Answers: Jehovah's Witnesses*, published by Catholic Answers Press.

157 "Is It Proper to Worship Jesus?" *Awake!*, April 8, 2000, 27. Available online at: http://wol.jw.org/en/wol/d/r1/lp-e/102000250.

158 "The Bible describes Michael as *the archangel*, implying that he alone bears that designation. Hence, it is reasonable to conclude that Jehovah God has delegated to one, and only one, of his heavenly creatures full authority over all other angels" (ibid.). "Is Jesus the Archangel Michael?" *The Watchtower*, April 1, 2010, 19. Available online at: http://wol.jw.org/en/wol/d/r1/lp-e/102002085.

159 Ibid.

160 Morna Hooker, *The Gospel According to Saint Mark* (Grand Rapids: Baker Academic, 1991), 140.

161 Robert M. Bowman Jr. and J. Ed Komoszewski, *Putting Jesus in His Place: The Case for the Deity of Christ* (Grand Rapids: Kregel Publications, 2007), 141.

162 Does God Have a Name?" *The Watchtower*, February 1, 2009, 6. Available online at: http://wol.jw.org/en/wol/d/r1/lp-e/2009082.

163 In the Old Testament, God's name is spelled with the consonants YHWH, known as the *tetragrammaton*. Over time the practice of respectfully not speaking the name caused the original pronunciation of the name to be lost, but Jewish sources have not accepted the pronunciation "Jehovah." The rendering of "Jehovah" came about in the eleventh century, when monks combined the Latin rendering of the tetragrammaton, with the vowels in the word *Adonai*, which gave us *Jah-hov-ai*, or Jehovah.

164 Although Mormons call themselves a "church," strictly speaking they are not a church because they do not possess valid holy orders or even valid beliefs about central Christian doctrines like the Trinity. But for sake of simplicity, I use the term "church" to describe their organization. Also, in 2018 their president Russell Nelson released a statement expressing a preference for people to call that church by its full name and no longer by any "Mormon" nickname. In my own writings on the subject, I will still use terms like *Mormon* and *LDS* for readability and because I don't think they're offensive. In conversations with individual Mormons, I'd recommend following their lead about which terms they prefer, since not all of them may agree with the new change.

Chapter 11
Our Eldest Brother

165 Gordon B. Hinkley, "We Look to Christ" *Ensign* (May 2002). Available online at: https://www.lds.org/ensign/2002/05/we-look-to-christ?lang=eng.

166   St. Athanasius said, "[W]e become by grace what God is by nature." (*De Incarnatione*, I). In other words, God gives us his divine life so that we *resemble* him but we never *become* him. Renowned historian of Christianity Jaroslav Pelikan says that the doctrine that men could become like God in holiness (what is called *theosis*) was, among people like Athanasius, "not to be viewed as analogous to classical Greek theories about the promotion of human beings to divine rank, and in that sense not to be defined by natural theology at all; on such errors they pronounced their 'Anathema!'" Jarolslav Pelikan, *Christianity and Classical Culture: The Metamorphosis of Natural Theology in the Christian Encounter with Hellenism* (Yale University Press, 1995), 318. In other words, the Church Fathers would not have recognized the Mormon doctrine of exaltation as being a variation of their doctrine of *theosis*. Instead, they would have considered it heresy.

167   The Mormon sacred text *Doctrine and Covenants* describes Jesus telling Joseph Smith, the founder of the Mormon faith, "I was in the beginning with the Father, and am the Firstborn; And all those who are begotten through me are partakers of the glory of the same, and are the church of the Firstborn. Ye were also in the beginning with the Father; that which is Spirit, even the Spirit of truth" (93:31–33).

168   "Origin of Man" *Improvement Era*, November 1909, 75–81. Available online at: https://www.lds.org/ensign/2002/02/the-origin-of- man?lang=eng.

169   Joseph Smith Jr., "The King Follett Sermon," *Ensign*, May 1971, 13. Available online at: https://www.lds.org/ensign/1971/04/the-king-follett-sermon?lang=eng.

170   Joseph Smith said of the Trinity, "[T]hree in one, and one in three! It is a curious organization. . . . All are to be crammed into one God, according to sectarianism. It would make the biggest God in all the world. He would be a wonderfully big God— he would be a giant or a monster." *Teachings of the Prophet Joseph Smith*, 372. But each person of the Trinity is not a *part* of God. Instead, each member *is* God, and because of this each member of the Trinity deserves the same level of worship, including the second person of the Trinity who became the man Jesus Christ.

171   For a more extended discussion of this argument for the existence of the traditional monotheistic God see Trent Horn. *Answering Atheism: How to Make the Case for God with Logic and Charity* (San Diego: Catholic Answers Press, 2013), 123–136.

172   Robert Karl Gnuse, *No Other Gods: Emergent Monotheism in Israel* (Sheffield: Sheffield Phoenix Press, 1997), 84.

173   *Letter to the Magnesians* 8:1.

174   Eric Shuster, *Catholic Roots, Mormon Harvest* (Springville, UT: Cedar Fort, Inc: 2009), 62.

175   *The Shepherd* 2:1.

176   This passage is so damaging to people who deny the Trinity and the divinity of Christ that some, like Jehovah's Witnesses, mistranslate it to say Jesus created "all other things," even though the Greek words for other (*heteros* and *allos*) are not in the original text.

177   Other critics cite Revelation 3:14 because it refers to Jesus as "the beginning of God's creation." But in Revelation 3:14, the Greek word translated "be- ginning," or *arche*, can also mean *ruler, source*, or *origin*. Indeed, in Revelation 21:6 the Father calls himself "the beginning," but this does not mean the Father had a literal beginning. What this verse means is that Jesus is the *source* of all creation.

178   Gene L. Green, *The Letters to the Thessalonians* (Grand Rapids, MI: Wm. B. Eerdmans, 2002), 176.

179   *Dialogue with Trypho*, 62.

Chapter 12
The Father in Disguise

180 Ibid., 56.

181 "Tertullian said of the traditional doctrine of the Trinity, "this rule of faith has come down to us from the beginning of the gospel, even before any of the older heretics, much more before Praxeas, a pretender of yesterday." *Against Praxeas*, 2.

182 *Sermon 2*, 2.

183 *Against Praxeas, 22*.

184 *First Apology*, 61.

185 See also Douglas McCready, *He Came Down from Heaven: The Preexistence of Christ and the Christian Faith* (Downer's Grove, IL: InterVarsity Press, 2005).

186 A.T. Robertson, *Word Pictures in the New Testament* (Nashville, TN: Broadman Press, 1932), 4.

187 Mark McNeil, *All in the Name* (El Cajon, CA: Catholic Answers Press, 2018), 87–88.

188 David K. Bernard, *The Oneness of God* (Weldon Spring, MO: Pentecostal Publishing House, 1986), 90. Cited in McNeil, 107.

189 *Against Praxeas, 25*.

Chapter 13
"Gay-Affirming" Savior

190 "President Jimmy Carter Authors New Bible Book, Answers Hard Biblical Questions." Interview with Paul Brandeis Raushenbush, *The Huffington Post*, March 19, 2012. Available online at: https://www.huffingtonpost.com/2012/03/19/president-jimmy-carter-bible-book_n_1349570.html.

191 "Jesus affirmed a gay couple" available online at: http://www.wouldjesusdiscriminate.org/biblical_evidence/gay_couple.html.

192 John Byron, "Did Jesus Heal a Centurion's Same-Sex Partner?" *The Biblical World*, August 9, 2012. Available online at: http://thebiblicalworld.blogspot.com/2012/08/did-jesus-heal-centurions-same-sex.html.

193 For a reply to attempts to revise St. Paul's teachings on this subject see Trent Horn, "The Bible on Homosexual Behavior," *Catholic Answers Magazine Online*, May 1, 2015. Available online at: https://www.catholic.com/magazine/print-edition/the-bible-on-homosexual-behavior.

194 Gene Robinson, *God Believes in Love: Straight Talk about Gay Marriage* (Toronto: Random House, 83–84).

195 It's true that verse nineteen refers to a ceremonial law related to menstruation, but this prohibition merely forbids sex during menstruation. The other verses in this section describe moral evils that are "defilements," "profane," "perverted," and—in the case of same-sex behavior—"abominations." Illicit sex with a menstruating woman is never called an "abomination" or a "perversion" like the other moral crimes listed alongside it.

196 John Boswell, *Christianity, Social Tolerance, and Homosexuality* (Chicago: University of Chicago Press, 1981), 100–102.

197 For a comprehensive list see Robert A.J. Gagnon, *The Bible and Homosexual Practice: Texts and Hermeneutics* (Nashville, TN: Abingdon Press, 2001), 118–119.

198 Some revisionists claim that homosexual behavior had nothing to do with the destruction of Sodom and Gomorrah. They say that Sodom's sin was inhospitality and pride (Ezekiel 16:48–49). But Genesis 13:13 says that even before the angel's

suffered "inhospitality" (if that's what you call it), the men of Sodom were wicked and sinned greatly against the Lord. The New Testament also describes the sexual nature of Sodom's sin. 2 Peter 2:7 says God rescued Lot, who was "greatly distressed by the licentiousness of the wicked." Jude 7 says, "Sodom and Gomor'rah acted immorally and indulged in unnatural lust." Some revisionists say that Jude is condemning the men of Sodom only for seeking after the strange flesh of angels but the men of Sodom thought the visitors were also men and did not know they were angels (Gen. 19:5). For Jude, *sarkos heteras* meant flesh that differed from the men of Sodom—flesh that differed from what those men should have naturally pursued: it meant male flesh. Finally, while it's true that Genesis 19 does not explicitly condemn consensual same-sex relations, neither does it exclude the fact that part of Sodom's immoral reputation came from its males engaging in same-sex intercourse.

199 John Boswell, *Christianity, Social Tolerance, and Homosexuality* (Chicago: University of Chicago Press, 1981), 100.

200 Robert A.J. Gagnon, *The Bible and Homosexual Practice: Texts and Hermeneutics* (Nashville, TN: Abingdon Press, 2001), 48.

201 Ibid., 209.

202 Patrick Cheng, *Radical Love: Introduction to Queer Theology* (New York: Seabury Books, 2011), x.

203 See the Babylonian Talmud tractates Gittin 90 A-B.

204 See also Jimmy Akin, "Did Jesus Say Adultery Is Grounds for Divorce?" *Catholic Answers Magazine Online*, July 01, 2000. Available online at: https://www.catholic. com/magazine/print-edition/did-jesus-say-adultery-is-grounds-for-divorce.

205 The text says, "I, Shelamzion, daughter of Joseph Qebshan of Ein Gedi, with you, Eleazar son of Hananiah who had been the husband before this time, that this is from me to you a bill of divorce and release." Cited in David Instone-Brewer, *Divorce and Remarriage in the Bible: The Social and Literary Context* (Grand Rapids, Wm. B. Eerdmans, 2002), 88.

206 Ibid., 89.

Chapter 14
Socialist Liberator

207 Elliot Kaufman, "Stern Dining Should Not Honor Mass Murderers," *The Stanford Review* (2012). Available online at: https://stanfordreview.org/stern-dining-should-not-honor-mass-murderers/.

208 Barbara Ehrenreich, *Nickel and Dimed: On (Not) Getting By in America* (New York: Henry Holt and Company, 2001), 68.

209 Alvaro de Juana and Elise Harris, "Pope Francis apparently not amused by 'communist crucifix.'" *Catholic News Agency*, July 09, 2015. Available online at: https://www.catholicnewsagency.com/news/pope-francis-apparently-not-amused-by-communist-crucifix-33337.

210 *Quadragesimo Anno*, 120.

211 Kenneth Leech, "Socialism" in *The Oxford Companion to Christian Thought*, ed. Adrian Hastings et al. (New York: Oxford University Press, 2000), 677.

212 Lawrence Reed, *Render Unto Ceasar: Was Jesus a Socialist?* (Atlanta, GA: Foundation for Economic Education, 2015), Kindle edition.

213 "By and large, only the dishonorable rich, the dishonorable nonelites, and those

beyond the pale of public opinion (such as city elites, governors, regional kings) could accumulate wealth with impunity. This they did in a number of ways, notably by trading, tax collecting, and money lending. . . . In the first century [these methods] would all be considered dishonorable and immoral forms of usury." Bruce Malina, *The New Testament World: Insights from Cultural Anthropology* (Louisville, KY: Westminster John Knox Press, 2001), 104–105.

214 "Estimates of the total number of all Christian martyrs in the former Soviet Union are about 12 million." James Nelson, *Psychology, Religion, and Spirituality* (New York: Springer, 2009), 427.

215 George Ritzer, *Essentials of Sociology* (Los Angeles: Sage Publications, 2016), 289.

216 Gustavo Gutierrez, *A Theology of Liberation* (Maryknoll, NY: Orbis Books, 1988), 157.

217 Jean Galot, *Jesus, Our Liberator: A Theology of Redemption* (Chicago: Franciscan Herald Press, 1982), 82.

218 Quoted in Paul Sigmund. *Liberation Theology at the Crossroads: Democracy or Revolution?* (New York: Oxford University Press, 1990), 163.

219 Andrea Gagliarducci, "Cardinal: Liberation Theology needed separation from Marxism," *Catholic News Agency*, February 25, 2014. Available online at: https://www.catholic-newsagency.com/news/cardinal-liberation-theology-needed-separation-from-marxism.

220 "Pie in sky when you die" is a lyric from Joe Hill's satirical 1911 song, "The Preacher and the Slave," which parodies lyrics from the 1868 hymn, "The Sweet By-and-By." Hill considered groups like the Salvation Army as focusing too much on heaven and not being willing to organize for workers' rights.

221 "Only In Christ Will Man Find Total Salvation." Available online at: http://www.vatican.va/jubilee_2000/magazine/documents/ju_mag_01041998_p-26_en.html.

222 C.S. Lewis, *The World's Last Night and Other Essays* (Orlando, FL: Harcourt, 1987), 98.

Chapter 15
Flawed & Failed Prophet

223 John Loftus, "At Best Jesus Was a Failed Apocalyptic Prophet," *The Christian Delusion: Why Faith Fails*, ed. John Loftus (Amherst, NY: Prometheus Books, 2010), 316.

224 Stephanie Coontz, "'Family Values' That Christ Wouldn't Recognize," the *New York Times*, July 13, 2012. Available online at: https://www.nytimes.com/roomfordebate/2012/04/24/are-family-values-outdated/family-values-that-christ-wouldnt-recognize.

225 Mike Nappa, *The Jesus Survey: What Christian Teens Really Believe and Why* (Grand Rapids, MI: Baker Books, 2012), 32–33.

226 "If we learn to understand the content of the Transfiguration story in these terms—as the irruption and inauguration of the messianic age—then we are also able to grasp the obscure statement that Mark's Gospel inserts between Peter's confession and the teaching on discipleship, on one hand, and the account of the transfiguration, on the other." Joseph Ratzinger, *Jesus of Nazareth* (San Francisco: Ignatius Press, 2008), 317.

227 Some scholars who deny Christ's divinity say the evangelists added his prophecies about the destruction of the temple after the fact, but miraculous abilities were not needed to see that tensions between the Jewish people and Rome could lead to a full-scale conflict. Josephus even records another Jesus named Jesus Ben Ananias who would not stop publicly saying, "Woe, woe to Jerusalem" and preaching its imminent destruction (*Jewish War*, 6.5.3.)

228   Fr. William Most, *The Consciousness of Christ* (Front Royal: Christendom College Press, 1980), 60.

229   *Jewish War*, 5.5.5.

230   *Jewish War*, 5.5.4.

231   Douglas R. Edwards, *Religion & Power: Pagans, Jews, and Christians in the Greek East* (New York: Oxford University Press, 1996), 139.

232   Dan Barker, *Godless: How an Evangelical Preacher Became One of America's Leading Atheists* (Berkeley, CA: Ulysses Press, 2008), 179.

233   Craig A. Evans, *Word Biblical Commentary Vol. 34b, Mark 8:27–16:20* (Grand Rapids, MI: Zondervan, 2018), Kindle edition.

234   Mark J. Keown, *Jesus in a World of Colliding Empires, Volume Two: Mark 8:30–16:8 and Implications: Mark's Jesus from the Perspective of Power and Expectations* (Eugene, OR: Wipf and Stock, 2018), 105.

235   Craig S. Keener, *The Historical Jesus of the Gospels* (Grand Rapids, MI: Wm. B. Eerdmans, 2009), 205.

236   Some people argue that Christ was not omniscient in his divine intellect because he said concerning his Second Coming (which pertains to the Father's eternal plans), "But of that day or that hour no one knows, not even the angels in heaven, nor the Son, but only the Father" (Mark 13:32). Throughout Church history, some Church Fathers and theologians ascribed real ignorance to the Son on this matter while others said this was a mental reservation and Jesus just meant he does not know the time for the sake of revealing it (though he surely knows it). From the late Middle Ages, the *Catechism* says of this verse and a similar one in Acts 1:7, "What he admitted to not knowing in this area, he elsewhere declared himself not sent to reveal," (CCC 474), which implies that Jesus only knew in his human knowledge the Father's plans that he was meant to reveal and so he did not know this fact about his second coming. For more see Jimmy Akin, "The Magisterium and the Human Knowledge of Christ," *Catholic World Report*, March 18, 2016. Available online at: https://www.catholicworldreport.com/2016/03/18/the-magisterium-and-the-human-knowledge-of-christ/.

237   Pope Benedict XVI, *Jesus of Nazareth: The Infancy Narratives* (New York: Image, 2012), 127. Cited in Jimmy Akin, "What if Jesus played Basketball?" jimmyakin.com, March 21, 2017. Available online at: http://jimmyakin.com/2017/03/what-if-jesus-played-basketball.html.

238   "Like us in all things except sin," General Audience, February 3, 1988.

239   "The minds of demons are utterly perverted from the divine wisdom, they at times form their opinions of things simply according to the natural conditions of the same. Nor are they ever deceived as to the natural properties of anything; but they can be misled with regard to supernatural matters; for example, on seeing a dead man, they may suppose that he will not rise again, or, on beholding Christ, they may judge him not to be God (*Summa Theologiae*, I:58:5).

240   This same teaching is echoed in the *Catechism* (CCC 467) and also appears in a general audience Pope John Paul II gave on February 3, 1988 called *Semejante en Todo a Nosotros, Menos en el Pecado*, or "like us in all things except sin."

Chapter 16
Prosperity Preacher

241   For an extended historical discussion of this theology, see Kate Bowler, *Blessed: A History of the American Prosperity Gospel* (Oxford: Oxford University Press, 2018).

242 David Van Biema and Jeff Chu, "Does God Want You to Be Rich?" *Time* magazine, September 10, 2006. Available online at: http://content.time.com/time/magazine/article/0,9171,1533448-2,00.html.

243 Oral Roberts, *The Miracle of Seed-Faith* (Tulsa, Oral Roberts Ministry, 1982), Kindle edition.

244 Kenneth Copeland, *The Laws of Prosperity* (Forth Worth, TX: Kenneth Copeland Productions, 1974), 67.

245 Gloria Copeland, *God's Will Is Prosperity* (Harrison House Publishers, 2012), 54.

246 Leroy Thompson, *Money Cometh to the Body of Christ* (Darrow, LA: Ever Increasing Word Ministries, 1996), 16.

247 Kathleen Elkins, "Billionaires Warren Buffett and Bill Gates have similar ideas about how much money you should leave your kids," cnbc.com, September 26, 2016. Available online at: https://www.cnbc.com/2016/09/26/warren-buffett-bill-gates-have-similar-ideas-on-how-much-money-to-leave-kids.html.

248 Creflo Dollar, "Prayer: Your Path to Success" cited in David W. Jones and Russell S. Woodbridge, *Health, Wealth, and Happiness: How the Prosperity Gospel Overshadows the Gospel of Christ* (Grand Rapids: Kregel Publications, 2017), 147.

249 David Croteau, *Urban Legends of the New Testament: 40 Common Misconceptions* (Nashville, TN: B&H Publishing Group, 2015), 63.

250 John Blake, "Passions over 'prosperity gospel': Was Jesus wealthy?" CNN.com, December 25, 2009. Available online at: http://www.cnn.com/2009/LIVING/wayoflife/12/25/RichJesus/index.html.

251 David Fiensy, *Christian Origins and the Ancient Economy* (Eugene, OR: Cascade Books, 2014), 33.

Chapter 17
A Sacrifice Only for Some

252 The debate can be viewed online at: https://www.youtube.com/watch?v=72TRODe8BdA.

253 Arthur W. Pink. *Studies in the Scriptures*, Vol. 7 (Lafayette, IN: Sovereign Grace Publishers, 2005,) 212.

254 For an in-depth reply to these verses see I. Howard Marshall, "Universal Grace and Atonement in the Pastoral Epistles," in *The Grace of God and the Will of Man: A Case for Arminianism*, ed. Clark H. Pinnock (Grand Rapids, MI: Zondervan, 1989), 57–63.

255 Richard Carrier, "Two Examples of Faulty Bible Scholarship," *infidels.org* (1999). Available online at: https://infidels.org/library/modern/richard_carrier/bible.html.

256 David Nelson, "The Design, Nature, and Extent of the Atonement" in *Calvinism: A Southern Baptist Dialogue*, eds. Brad J. Waggoner and E. Ray Clendenen (Nashville, TN: B&H Publishing, 2008), 127–128.

257 Mel Shoemaker, *The Theology of the Four Gospels* (Bloomington, IN: Thomas Nelson, 2011), 253.

258 I owe this observation to Jimmy Akin. St. John Chrysostom, *Homilies on the Gospel of John*, 81.2.

259 James R. White, *Drawn by the Father* (Lindenhurst, NY: Great Christian Books, 2000), 26.

Chapter 18
The Anti-Catholic with No Face

260 Tony Miano and Matt Slick, "Is the Sinner's Prayer Biblical or Not?" Christian Apologetics and Research Ministry (CARM). Available online at: https://carm.org/

sinners-prayer. The prayer's origin in the early twentieth century is documented in Paul Harrison's doctoral dissertation on the subject. Available online at: https://digital.library.sbts.edu/handle/10392/4153.

261 The tract can be viewed online at: https://www.chick.com/products/tract?stk=0074&Store=True.

262 Joachim Jeremias, *The Eucharistic Words of Jesus* (New York: Charles Scribner and Sons, 1966), 255.

263 As I note in my book *The Case for Catholicism*, "Jesus was instituting a fulfillment of the Passover, whose celebration 'made present' in a mystical way the events of the Exodus. Therefore, through the new Passover the Eucharist would make Christ's sacrifice present for all future believers. According to the non-Catholic scholar Anthony Thiselton, 'The Passover *Seder* enables Jewish households *to participate in* the deliverance of the Passover *as if they were "there."* The Eucharist enables Christians to participate in the deliverance of the cross *as if they were "there."* They are *contemporaneous sharers in the drama'"* [emphasis in original]. Trent Horn, *The Case for Catholicism: Answers to Classic and Contemporary Protestant Objections* (San Francisco: Ignatius Press, 2017), 162.

264 Brant Pitre, *Jesus and the Jewish Roots of the Eucharist* (New York: Doubleday, 2011), 144–145.

265 This was part of an exchange MacArthur had on the December 2, 2018 episode of *The Ben Shapiro Show*, available online at: https://www.youtube.com/watch?v=F-ofKxfYqGw. I also analyse MacArthurs arguments at fuller length in Trent Horn, "Refuting a Pastor's 'Dark Ages' Myths," *Catholic Answers Online Magazine*, December 04, 2018. Available online at: https://www.catholic.com/magazine/online-edition/refuting-a-pastors-dark-ages-myths.

266 *Treatise 1*.

267 *Epistle to the Smyrnaeans*, 8.

268 The Protestant author D.A. Carson says, "Only "church" (*ekklesia* in the singular) is used for the congregation of all believers in one city, never "churches"; one reads of churches in Galatia [a region, not a city] but of *the church* [emphasis added] in Antioch or Jerusalem or Ephesus." D.A. Carson, "Church Authority," in *Evangelical Dictionary of Theology*, 2nd ed. (Grand Rapids, MI: Baker, 2001), 250.

Appendix:
Counterfeit Christs in Politics

269 *Donum Veritatis*, 24.

270 Ibid.

271 *Forming Consciences for Faithful Citizenship*, 33.

272 John L. Allen Jr., "Chaput in Philly swims against 'nostalgia and red ink'" *National Catholic Reporter*, September 14, 2012. Available online at: https://www.ncronline.org/news/parish/chaput-philly-swims-against-nostalgia-and-red-ink.

273 Erika Christakis, "Is Paul Ryan's Budget 'Un-Christian'?" *Time* magazine, August 14, 2012. Available online at: http://ideas.time.com/2012/08/14/why-paul-ryans-budget-unchristian/.

274 "The Bible and Taxes," *Wallbuilders*, December 31, 2016. Available online at: https://wallbuilders.com/the-bible-and-taxes/.

ABOUT THE AUTHOR

After his conversion to the Catholic faith, Trent Horn earned a master's degree in theology from Franciscan University of Steubenville, a master's degree in philosophy from Holy Apostles College, and is pursuing a master's degree in bioethics from the University of Mary.

As a staff apologist for Catholic Answers, he specializes in teaching Catholics to graciously and persuasively engage those who disagree with them. Trent models that approach each week on the radio program *Catholic Answers Live*, where he dialogues with atheists, pro-choice advocates, and other non-Catholic callers.

Trent is also an adjunct professor of apologetics at Holy Apostles College and the author of seven books, including *Answering Atheism*, *The Case for Catholicism*, and *Why We're Catholic: Our Reasons for Faith, Hope, and Love*.